Trans Forming Families:

Real Stories About Transgendered Loved Ones

Mary Boenke
Editor

Foreword by Robert Bernstein
Introduction by Jessica Xavier

TRANS FORMING FAMILIES:
Real Stories About Transgendered Loved Ones

Mary Boenke, Editor

Walter Trook Publishing
276 Date Street
Imperial Beach, CA 91932

Copy Editor - Daphne Reed
Art Work - Dean Mitchell
        Dennis/Romana Pernaa
        Dolores M. Dudley
        Lori Bowden

* Indicates change in names to protect
anonymity and privacy

Printed in the United States of America
January 1999

Library of Congress Card Catalogue Number: 98-89891
ISBN: 0-9663272-1-7

This book is lovingly dedicated

To our own new son
who has dared
be true to himself
and taught us so much,

To all those brave, dedicated
and pioneering transgendered persons
who have risked so much for
their own integrity and
for those to come, and

To all those courageous families,
open to ambiguity and new frontiers,
holding love more important
than social custom.

IN MEMORY

We wish to remember with love and gratitude three outstanding women whose sudden deaths this past year have saddened us immensely, and whose lives we wish to honor. These women were valiant, talented, dedicated persons, who were role models for the transgender community each in her own unique way.

DEE MCKELLAR, 1942 - 1997

Dee was a trans-activist, had worked and lobbied with the International Conference on Law and Employment Policy, and tutored young adults working toward their high school diploma .

JENNIFER LATEINER, 1973 - 1998

In additional to her professional accomplishments in computer software development, Jenni was overflowing with creativity, a contagious joy of life, and self-awareness and understanding far beyond her tender years.

JOANNA MCNAMARA, 1950 - 1998

Joanna was a talented attorney, dedicated to law reform and justice for all transgendered persons, struggling against both physical and psychological pain.

CONTENTS

PART 1 RAISING GENDER-VARIANT CHILDREN

PART II LEARNING FROM OUR CHILDREN OF ALL AGES

PART IV CRUCIAL OTHERS

* Pseudonym

PREFACE

This collection gradually took shape in my mind as I discovered how many families reject their transgendered loved ones and how little is published to help them. We, personally, have experienced the remarkably fulfilling double drama of both having an FTM (female-to-male) son and also finding a wonderful community of other families and individuals to help us through the process of learning, adjusting and growing. We wanted to share our experience and make available some positive family role models for those families who are struggling, in pain, with similar transgender issues. We know these happier family stories may be an uncomfortable contrast to the experiences of many transgender persons, but we hope these stories will help many families heal more quickly and truly embrace both their transgendered loved one and their own family trans formation.

My husband of forty-four years and I have three wonderful adult children. Two are married to just-right spouses and have produced five bouncy grandchildren. Our middle child came out to us as a lesbian twenty years ago after her freshman year at college, and again three years ago as a transsexual. Allen,* our new son, has legally changed his name, driver's license and other legal papers, and his career. He has ended a long-term love relationship, gained new friends, and gone through much of the sexual transition process, including counseling, trans support group, hormonal therapy and both "top surgery" (breast reduction), and a hysterectomy. We think he is enormously brave, admirably honest to self, friends and family about who he really is, and ever so commendable for the grace with which he has jumped off the seeming edge of the world into a brand new life.

In the process he has introduced us to a whole new world for which we have become eternally grateful. We have learned at least the basics about sexual transition, its severe risks and social, emotional and economic costs as well as the compelling and often long, excruciating inner experience that brings many persons to follow this course.

We have learned, as well, to question our culture's way of looking at many things as dichotomies - black and white, good and evil, straight and gay, even male and female. In reality, the world is more complex than we might prefer to think. There are, respectively, shades of gray, relatively better or worse courses of action, bisexuality, and now, we have learned, even a continuum between male and female. We are all somewhere on a variety of continua - between young and old, tall and short, smart and stupid, fat and thin, straight and gay, and even in our gender presentation, between macho and very feminine. In short, we have developed a greater appreciation for the beauty and diversity of nature, a much keener sensitivity to the vast array of our similarities and differences, and a sense of greater connectedness to all people. We are not so much different "in kind," but, truly, only "in degree."

While much has been written by, and about, the varieties of gender persons, their journeys, the current political process, even counseling, very little has been published about the corresponding journey, also often very difficult and painful, that parents, partners and other family members must make in order to maintain the relationship[1]. Of course, the process to acceptance is different and unique for each person and family. Yet, there are similarities; we can all learn from one another and be comforted by knowing we are not alone.

The writings collected here are mostly by mothers and partners or spouses, but also by fathers, siblings, grandparents and children of trans persons. One exception is by a crossdresser, about his mother's surprising response when he came out to her. The writings are about both male-to-female and female-to-male transsexuals, crossdressers, intersexed persons, children, youth and adults of all ages. They represent a great variety also, in the internal experiences of growing toward acceptance, in the degree of family support, and in the obstacles encountered externally along the way.

While parents are expected to continue to love and accept their children, no matter what, we are continually amazed at how many do not. We are equally surprised at the many marriages and love relationships that have survived one partner's sexual transition. Remember, when a husband changes from male to female, both the marriage and the spouse shift as well from straight to, ostensibly, lesbian. Or if one partner in a lesbian couple transitions the reverse is true. Often their whole community of friends also changes. Incredible as this must seem to some, we have come to know quite a few such couples whose bonds have not only continued, but seem to be stronger for the struggle. Some will readily explain that they did not fall in love with a body part, but with a person. As a parent, I have been comforted to know that there is, indeed, love after transition!

This collection varies as well in the style, experience and level of sophistication of writing. I have chosen to do relatively little editing and to preserve the writers' personalities as much as possible. Readers will no doubt identify more with some families and styles than with others. The writings are grouped by categories, albeit somewhat arbitrarily, to make finding parallels with the reader's situation more accessible.

We are particularly pleased to present some stories by parents of young gender-variant children as there is practically nothing available, in print, for these families. Most have been isolated and struggling alone for some time until their child's condition could even be identified. Some children were adamant about their "other" gender at surprisingly early ages. As yet, there is little appropriate treatment available, except perhaps some supportive counseling, for these children and their families. We deplore those treatment modalities which attempt to "cure" cross-gender expression, and probably only drive those needs underground to cause more pain later on. (Like a new friend of mine, who was squelched at age four for wanting a pretty dress, only to finally start cross-dressing at age fifty — after many painful years struggling to sort out his identity!) While some of these children seem destined to become transsexuals, we know they should not be categorized too soon, for some will grow up to be gay, lesbian, bi-sexual, or even straight.

Fortunately, we were able to include two stories about intersexed loved ones. I have only recently, myself, begun to understand and appreciate the variety of intersexuals, the tragedy that infancy and childhood so-called "normalizing" surgery can wreak on some lives, and the need to include this group in our support, education and advocacy work.

As a founder of the Transgender Special Outreach Network (TSON) within Parents, Families and Friends of Lesbians and Gays (PFLAG), I have found abundant support for my own journey. This experience has also led us to work toward identifying Transgender Coordinators in over 175 chapters, writing, marketing and selling over 12,000 copies of Our Trans Children[2], an introduction to trans issues, and thus educating other parents in many PFLAG chapters and elsewhere across the country. Our goal of making PFLAG officially transgender-inclusive was reached in September 1998.

Along the way we have met wonderfully resilient, resourceful and dedicated people, both trans persons and also their staunch allies, in many cities. We have all done countless speaking engagements at all levels, lobbied, written numerous articles, and told and retold our own stories, sent thousands of email posts, cried and laughed with each other along the way and felt magnificently enriched and rewarded for our work of love. In PFLAG we often say that many parents move beyond the usual stages of grief, even beyond acceptance, to a place of celebration. It's true!

The past few years have truly been an amazing learning experience, one I wouldn't have missed for anything!

Mary Boenke
Hardy, Virginia
October 1998

ACKNOWLEDMENTS

My husband and I wish to express our profound gratitude for years of experience with Parents, Families and Friends of Lesbians and Gays where we learned much about parental journeys into the world of sexual minorities, where we gained extraordinary friends around the country, and where we honed our helping and organizing skills.

We are immensely indebted to PFLAG's Transgendered Special Outreach Network (TSON), created only three years ago, and all the dedicated, resourceful, and ever so exceptional people, both trans folks and allies, who have contributed significantly to both my own trangendered education and to so many others in this country.

I, especially, want to thank PFLAG members Jessica Xavier, who drafted much of the Glossary and Transgender Resources (though I take responsibility for the final draft), Karen and Bob Gross, who do almost everything for TSON, Maggie Heineman, for her organizational and electronic communications skill, Just Evelyn, for daring to believe in and help her teenager transition, and last but definitely not least, Daphne Reed, for her sharp eye, professional help, and patience as my copy editor.

It is impossible to say too much for the contributors to this book. They are brave, resiliant, creative, loving, patient pioneers.

My husband has been a patient and loving supporter for forty-four years during my many projects, for which I love and appreciate him more — and now wish him well with his own creation-in-process. Our three adult children and their families have all added icing to our family cake as we work. Truly, our own family has been trans focused and trans formed.

FOREWORD

The stories in this book, in moving and inspiring fashion, confirm some of the most basic truths of humankind.

Perhaps the most important, typically honored more in the breach than the observance, is the truism enshrined in the Shakespearean admonition, "To thine own self be true." The path of integrity and self-discovery, however risky, can lift the human spirit to new levels of spontaneity, sensitivity and creativity. For anyone to realize their highest potential—be they straight, gay or trans; black, white, yellow or brown—they need first to be able to utter the simple words, "I am what I am, and that's OK."

But we live of course in a social climate that conditions us to think in quite different fashion. It teaches that we are what society as a whole deems us to be. It commands us to heed pre-ordained standards that determine how "successful," "attractive" or generally desirable we appear to others.

Foremost among these standards, these crimpers of the soul, are our stereotypical gender roles. Little boys shouldn't cry or show emotion. Little girls should be demure and passive. How many millions of personalities have been warped, and lives thereby ruined, by even these most simple of everyday strictures?

Imagine, then, the courage inherent in defying not merely the notion of gender roles, but the traditional concept of gender itself!

So this is a book about courage.

It also is a book about love and family values.

It foresees a day of fuller awareness, of recognition that we all are indeed unique. That the shape of our being is determined no more by our genitalia than by the color of our eyes. That the worth of our souls isn't measurable by handed-down norms.

In this exciting collection, the authors tell us that each of us is more than simply man or woman but, rather, a wonderful, awesome mosaic of richly interwoven qualities that, at bottom, defy gender assignment.

Don't read it if you want to go on believing that gender is a clear-cut, either/or, one-of- two-sizes-fits-all, proposition.

Robert Bernstein, author
Straight Parents/Gay Children
July 1998

INTRODUCTION

"What about your family?" It's a question I've heard at least a hundred times, and each time I've just had to answer it. As a peer educator, I've made over one hundred gender education presentations to colleges and universities, mental health and sexology groups, crisis centers and hotlines, and gay, lesbian and bisexual organizations in the Washington and Baltimore area. "What about your family?" is the one question I can count on getting asked, every time I get up in front of a group of strangers and out myself as a post-operative transsexual woman. And yet, I still struggle with the answer, even though it's now seven years after gender transition and five years after surgery. With the audience's eyes focused on my face, eagerly awaiting the answer, I swallow hard on the pain and summon the courage to reply as best I can. I usually give a short-hand answer to the sorrow of rejection and the joy of partial acceptance I experienced when, after thirty-eight years of living a lie, I finally accepted myself and told my family.

Losing half of my birth family in gender transition was extremely painful for me, and I am sure it also was painful for them, but sadly, this is a common experience for most trans people. That pain led me to PFLAG, and eventually to their Transgender Special Outreach Network (TSON). Here I found parents and grandparents, brothers and sisters, friends, spouses and partners of transsexual and transgendered men and women. Here I found a place to focus my energies on the many issues that families face when their son or daughter, brother or sister, spouse or partner, parent or grandchild tells them the words that no family member should ever want or expect to hear. Here in our steadily growing TSON trans family, we are developing at least some answers for the sudden rush of questions that follow in the wake of disclosure that one of our own is transgendered.

For almost all people, gender follows one's birth sex, and thus it's a given, quickly taken for granted. This one obvious fact facilitates a wall of ignorance, not only about trans people but also about gender itself. Gender is ubiquitous - it governs the full spectrum of human behaviors and yet almost all people are wholly unconscious of it. Gender also is an unspoken and unwritten social contract that all people enter into without really much discussion or debate. Gender in a heterosexist world is simply the way things are - for men and for women, and for boys and for girls.

But it's not that simple for trans people, many of whom spend half their lifetimes struggling to understand who they are, and the other half becoming who they feel they were meant to be all along. Ours is usually an internal war, which we keep hidden from others because of our shame, guilt, and isolation. In simple terms, it's a struggle for selfhood - to be finally, fully, human. Contrary to the conventional "wisdom," we trans people are not confused - we know who we are. It is human society that's confused by us, labeling the transcendence of sex and gender as mental disorders and our gender variance as a psychopathology. In time, if we are fortunate, we come to see our gender differences not as burdens but as special gifts. Indeed, I have come to regard my own transsexualism as a wondrous, spiritual voyage. But it has not been a voyage without storms.

And so, the question still begs, "What about your family?" Mary Boenke and her contributors have assembled a book of answers to that question. Every family is different, but most of those represented herein have struggled to come to terms of acceptance of their transgendered loved ones, as children, adolescents, and fully-grown adults. But there is so much more than mere struggle here, beyond the shame, guilt and confusion, and the simple difficulties of getting used to new names and pronouns. Parents grieving of the loss of their child, mixed with the joyous discovery of another child they never knew. Families learning new lessons from traveling vicariously with their transgendered voyagers through their new lives. Spouses and partners creating new understandings of committal relationships beyond the obsolete definitions and irrelevant legalities by their descriptions of what it means to love a changeling. Children and siblings coming to see their trans parents and trans siblings as unexpected blessings in their lives. There is indeed much to celebrate throughout these pages as these butterflies emerge transformed from their chrysalis to spread newly gendered wings over the world, held aloft by the love and courage of their families and their loved ones.

The stories in this book are, perhaps, the best examples of trans family members, since they are willing not only to accept but also to write about their exceptional children, siblings and even parents. As such, they are the first, brave ones to out themselves, out of love for their trans family members. In their own individual ways, they all have come to understand their trans loved one, fighting through much misinformation and massive stigmatization to obtain truthful, factual information about trans people. Of course, it was their determination to learn, to help, and to love them — no matter who they were or who they were becoming — that made the difference. It is that special love that marks PFLAGers everywhere.

But there are many other families still living in the shadow of the public's misunderstanding of transgendered people. Perhaps this book will find this way into their hands and open their hearts, as they discover themselves in these pages, in the personal struggles of these courageous contributors. Mary tells me that things are indeed getting better for transgendered people, and since she's my adoptive mom, I have to believe her! But we have so much more work to do, and so much farther to go, down this road so rarely traveled. I pray this book gets us to a future without fear that much faster.

Jessica Xavier
Kensington, Maryland
August 26, 1998

PART I

RAISING GENDER VARIANT CHILDREN:

TELL GRANDMA I'M A BOY
Florence Dillon*

My children, husband and I live with a golden retriever (male), a cat (female), and a cockatiel (gender indeterminate). Working to make the elementary school environment safe for our son has convinced me that public awareness of the realities of transgendered experience is critical for the healthy development and survival to adulthood of all gender-variant children.

My husband and I have two sons. Like most siblings, they're enmeshed in a love-hate relationship as rivals at home; they staunchly defend each other in the world outside. Alex, who just turned fourteen, is a classical musician and computer whiz. He's wired his room like a space station command center. He seems to have weathered puberty with ease, his voice is deeper, his personality composed.

Steve just turned eleven. His life revolves around rocketry, soccer, and improvising stand-up comedy routines in the kitchen. Still enjoying the comfortable androgyny of childhood, he's in denial about puberty being just around the corner. As his parents, we're concerned about the changes puberty will bring, because we know how distressing it will be for him to begin to develop breasts in middle school. And we're sure that, unless something is done to postpone or stop it, he will develop breasts and begin to menstruate, because this child, who feels and behaves in every way like an ordinary boy, has a normal female body.

When our second child was born, the doctor lifted the tiny, squirming baby so my husband, James, could see it clearly. I heard jubilation in James' voice as he announced, "It's Sarah!" That was the name we had decided to give our first baby girl. By the time we left the hospital 24 hours later, our daughter's birth certificate read "Sarah Elizabeth Anne," honoring both her grandmothers.

During her first year of life, Sarah ate, slept, and watched the world through wide, wise eyes. An avid breast-feeder, she was almost never out of my arms, and almost never made a sound. This observant stillness erupted into a storm of vigorous activity shortly after age one, however, accompanied by a torrent of grammatically complex sentences.

Her father and I were delighted with her verbal skills but terrified by her tendency to seek out the most hazardous physical challenges. Our experience with her more cautious older brother, Alex, hadn't prepared us for this toddler who would climb to the top of anything with handholds and, later, the preschooler who loved to jump from the tallest branch of our backyard tree down to the roof of the garage. But we were very proud of this child. I had always wanted a daughter who would define herself, who would grow to be strong and intelligent and independent. As a girl, I had been surrounded by capable women living purposeful lives, my mother and grandmothers and aunts, who loved me and made me feel very happy to be female. I grew up believing I could be and do whatever in the world I wanted, and one of the things I wanted most was to be a mother. Birthing this lively, fierce, and thoughtful little girl gave me a chance to hand down the powerful woman-centered heritage that had cradled me. I wanted to create a safe, warm nest where I could mother my daughter, then set her free to fly.

Sarah tested my resolve to set her free in a way I had never imagined. On her third birthday, she tore the wrapping paper from one of her grandmother's gifts and discovered a pink velvet dress trimmed in ribbons and white lace. I knew she wouldn't want to wear it. She hadn't voluntarily put on anything but pants since turning two, and this dress was totally impractical for playing the way Sarah played. Nevertheless, I was surprised by her reaction. She looked up, not unhappy, but puzzled and confused, and asked,

"Why is Grandma giving me a dress? Doesn't she know I'm not

the kind of girl who wears dresses?" Then, with an air of great satisfaction at finding the solution to her problem, she added, "Just tell Grandma I'm a boy." Initially, I assumed Sarah's announcement was simply an attempt to communicate a clothing preference in language she thought grownups would understand.

Then, a few weeks later, Sarah said she wanted us to call her "Steve." We thought this an odd but harmless request, and tried to remember to say "Steve" from time to time. Then we received a call from the Sunday school teacher who taught the three-year-olds at our church. She told us Sarah had asked her to cross out "Sarah" and write "Steve" on her name tag. We realized from this that the name "Steve" must be very important to Sarah, so we told the teacher it would be all right to call her "Steve" for the time being. At home, we talked to Sarah about the difference between a nickname like "Steve" and her real name. But in our neighborhood and on the playground at the park, Sarah began to introduce herself only as Steve. Within our family, she became more insistent that she was a boy. She never said "I want to be a boy" or "I wish I were a boy," but always, "I am a boy." She demanded we use masculine pronouns when referring to her. When we forgot or refused, her face would screw up in fury and exasperation, and the offending parent was likely to be pinched or kicked by this usually loving child. I stopped using pronouns altogether when Sarah was within earshot.

The teacher at our Montessori preschool wasn't as flexible as the Sunday school teacher. The children were learning to write their names, and "Sarah" was evidently the only name the teacher was willing to teach. This became an issue as Christmas approached. Four-year-old Sarah came home one day and asked how to spell "Steve" so she could sign her letter to Santa. When I cautioned that Santa might not be able to find our house if the name on the letter wasn't correct, she looked at me scornfully. "Santa knows where I live, Mommy. He knows my name is Steve."

I decided it was time to seek professional help. I had no idea why Sarah was convinced it was better to be a boy. Surely someone could tell me what I was doing wrong. And it must be something I was doing, or failing to do, because the children were in my care twenty-four hours a day. No one else had as many opportunities to influence them. My husband was successfully pursuing a corporate career that required his attention eleven or twelve hours a day, and I, very much by choice after fifteen years of work and academia, was a full-time mom. Our single-earner lifestyle, unusual in the nineteen-nineties, fulfilled the nostalgic fantasy of nuclear family life in the nineteen-fifties. I baked whole-wheat bread, cooked organically-grown vegetables, read aloud to my children every day, and volunteered in Alex's first-grade classroom two mornings each week when Sarah was in preschool.

My first call for help was to our state university's human development department. When I described my child and our family's situation, the "human development specialist" who took the call laughed reassuringly and said, "Don't worry about a thing. Your child has a great imagination. Lots of bright, creative kids try out different roles at this age. She'll grow out of it." With relief, I took her advice, stopped worrying, and waited for her to grow out of it. For the next couple of years, I supported my child's wish to be called Steve. I no longer made her unhappy by insisting, "You're a girl." Instead I said, "You have a girl's body, though Mommy and Daddy know you feel like a boy."

But I still felt responsible for my second child's not being able to accept that she was a girl, and set out to correct whatever misapprehensions she might have about becoming a woman. Because being a mother was such a joy for me, I told Sarah that what was wonderful about being a girl is that girls can grow up and have babies of their own. Hearing this, Sarah's face darkened. She shuddered and said, "I don't want to talk about that." She asked if everyone had to get married and have babies when they grew up.

When told no, of course not, she relaxed and said she was always going to live in our house with Alex.

By age five, Sarah had given all her dresses to a neighbor girl of the same age who loved dressing up. She wouldn't put on any item of clothing without first asking if it was made for a boy or a girl. Only boys' clothes would do. For Sarah, having an older brother ensured plenty of boys' hand-me-downs. That saved me the discomfort of shopping often for my daughter in the boys' departments of clothing stores. Even when Sarah wasn't with me, I felt compelled to confess to sales clerks that I was buying these shirts and pants and sport coats for my daughter who evidently thought it was better to be a boy. For some reason, I believed I owed perfect strangers an explanation of something I couldn't explain to myself.

Since traditional feminine dress and behavioral expectations were so distasteful to Sarah, I began a campaign to separate these "cultural trappings" from the biological fact of being female. I wanted Sarah to know she could be whatever kind of woman she wanted to be; she had the right to define herself as a person without regard to anyone else's expectations. Not only did she not have to get married and have children, but she would never have to put on a dress or makeup or wear her hair in any particular style unless she wanted to. She could pursue any kind of work she wanted. She could continue to be physically active and competitive all her life. I looked for children's books with strong female protagonists. Not at all athletic myself, I made friends with active, "outdoorsy" women who could be better role models than I for this sports-minded kid. Whenever a woman was mentioned in the news for any type of achievement, I trumpeted it loudly for Sarah's ears. To encourage our child to develop a well-rounded self-image, James would tell Sarah how pretty she was at the same time we were congratulating her on her strength and intelligence. We had read somewhere that the most successful professional women remember their fathers' recognizing and valuing their attractiveness as well as their intellectual accomplishments.

One day, after years of exposure to our "women can do anything" message, my seven-year-old turned to me with tearful eyes and said, "Mommy, you only like girls." Suddenly, I realized that everything I'd been doing to help my child feel good about herself had instead made him feel that I didn't accept or love who he really was. My child was Steve, a wonderfully creative, articulate, and very patient boy who had been waiting his whole life for his parents to see him.

Today, Steve is known as a boy by his classmates. He ís serving as president of the fifth grade and holds school records for push-ups and sit-ups. A very supportive administrator solved the classic bathroom problem by establishing single-person rest rooms for Steve's class. Instead of labeling them "boys" and "girls," there ís one for "kids" and one for "adults." The principal of the middle school Steve will attend next year has agreed to list him as a boy on all school documents. I'm writing this under a pseudonym to protect his privacy.

So we've come to the brink of puberty, when the disconnect between biology and gender threatens the psychological health Steve has so buoyantly maintained since his family acknowledged his reality and began to advocate for him in the world at large. It has been more than eight years since our three-year-old first said, "Just tell Grandma I'm a boy." That message has never varied.

We've learned to listen to our child. He's the only expert on his own experience. And, although his parents and older brother find it helpful to describe him as transgendered, Steve doesn't refer to himself that way. As far as Steve is concerned, he ís simply a boy.

I NEED TO BE A GIRL
Just Evelyn*

I am a cancer data specialist, and electrologist. I spend my free time doing public speaking and coordinating a transgender support group, "Transfamily San Diego". I am also involved in community theater and other local civic projects.

"I need to talk to you Mom. I have something to tell you, but I'm afraid you won't love me any more." My fifteen-year-old son lay down beside me on the bed in our usual family conference tradition. The children knew they had my undivided attention when I was already in bed.

I assured him that no matter what he told me, I would still love him. He hemmed and hawed and I thought he might be going to tell me he was gay. I had hoped such a conversation would take place sometime so that we could get involved in the gay community support system. But he had something entirely different on his mind.

He said, "I need to be a girl. I am a girl inside. I like boys but as a woman would, not the gay way. I have felt this way for years, and you know how feminine I am."

So this was what he had been upset about the last few months. At first I did not know what to say. I hugged him and thought, "Oprah Winfrey, where are you?" I rarely watched television, and daytime talk shows even less, so I had not been exposed to this issue before. Everything seemed to move in slow motion. I felt my life was taking a definite turn. I knew it would never be the same again.

Mind's Eye

A few months into the transition, a close friend was visiting when Danielle came exuberantly through the living room in her girlish, teenage manner.

After she was gone, I asked my friend, "Isn't she just the cutest thing?" His answer echoed in my ears for days. "In my mind's eye," he said, "I still see the boy I used to know."

Again and again that phrase went through my head. I had retrained my mind's eye so that now I only saw the girl, but I understood his reaction. In the beginning, even though my real eye could see the girl, my old brain would spit out male pronouns. After that experience, I could better understand why some parents have trouble allowing their children to grow up and change. In their minds they still have the image of a beloved toddler, an innocent seven or eight-year-old, or a rebellious teenager. It takes some time for the mind's eye to replace the youthftil image with a new picture of the adult. This may explain why a husband does not notice a new hairstyle, or why the family doesn't notice grandma's wrinkles. It is even more difficult to replace the old image with one of the opposite gender.

Since I saw Danielle everyday, my mind's eye had been retrained until I no longer saw the little boy, but only a lovable teenage girl. It was more difficult for Danielle's relatives to retrain their minds when they saw her infrequently or only in pictures.

Even though our eyes had seen the same person, my friend still saw the boy that used to be, whereas I just saw jubilant daughter.

Coming Out At School

Everything went smoothly for Danielle for almost a year before she became aware of the rumors about her. One girl even asked her if she had already had sex reassignment surgery. Danielle countered with, "That's a stupid question to ask anyone."

After the vice-principal (of the school she was attending, while living with her brother) called me, any hope of concentrating on my job was gone so I called Danielle right away. She said she had not called me because she did not want to worry me. "Anyway, she assured me, "It's no big deal."

She told me more about the circumstances leading up to her revelation. For a sociology class she wrote an autobiography, bu without revealing the truth, she knew it made no sense. She was sad that she could not reveal her real self, especially when she received a D on the paper. After much consideration, and all on her own, she decided to ask permission to make an announcement near the end of the class period. It was then that she told her story to her classmates and the teacher, then left immediately since it was near the end of the school day.

Within five minutes the story had spread throught the whole school. As soon as the principal and vice-principal heard, they visited her at home to see if she was all right and was not alone. Her brother, Ben, was already there, for one of Danielle's friends had called to warn him that Danielle might need him. The school representatives talked with Ben and Danielle for some time, then returned to the school, at which time the vice-principal called me. Even after talking to the kids, he could not quite believe that Danielle had once been a boy.

While she was telling me of all that had taken place, she kept reassuring me. "It's no big deal," she said, Everything is going to be fine, so just don't worry."

"I'm your mother, that's my job."

I wanted to get in the car, drive eight hours to Flagstaff and bring her home to safety, but I realized that I could not give her safety anywhere. She had to work through this for herself. She could either be proud and brave sticking it out or move to another new place and keep her mouth shut, thus denying part of who she is.

When I called a friend for support, he said, "You should be proud of her. She is turning out to be an activist just like her mother, and I didn't expect any less of her, for I have seen in her the courage and

11

determination to be herself."

I called the vice-principal the next day to tell him that Danielle thought everything was going to be fine. I learned that he had a meeting with Danielle's teachers to let them know about the situation, and to request their help to assure that she was not made fun of nor harassed in any way.

But he had a question. "Is the surgery complete so I can say that she is legally a female?"

That was an important question since she was in a girl's gym class. I assured him that she was legally a female. I also told him I would send him a packet of information about transsexuals.

I said, "Be proud of her for me."

He added, "We are all proud of her."[3]

~~~~~~~~~~

I see a beautiful butterfly emerging. The caterpillar was nice and I miss him, but the butterfly is so gentle, so peaceful, so softly radiant, that I almost don't remember the warm, fuzzy, little guy. The butterfly will be so wonderful once her wings are fully spread into the sun. (Jackie Greer, "A Spouse Speaks" from *Trans Forming Families*)

IS THE JOURNEY WORTH THE PAIN?
Barbara Lantz

I've been a single mother for fifteen years, and dealt with my child's issues alone until last year when I entered my first lesbian relationship. I'm 47, live in Seattle, and am a Health Information Manager in a not-for-profit community mental health center that provides both outpatient and inpatient services.

What mother hasn't dreamed of having a little girl? When my daughter Jenny was born my dream came true - I had my little girl. In a favorite picture of her, she is wearing a blue flowered dress with lace and a full petticoat. She is laughing happily. She looked like my perfect dream. But there was a football helmet on her head.

As time went on, the billowy dresses and flowers disappeared. Instead, Jenny dressed herself in baseball gear and overalls. She climbed fences and couldn't be found where she was supposed to be. She was loud, energetic and loved rough and tumble games. She made me shake my head and say "I have a tomboy." O.K., many mothers have tomboys and love them dearly, right?

By mid-adolescence it was clear that Jenny was more than a tomboy. As a 16-year-old "dyke", she was so extreme in appearance that her role model was James Dean. She couldn't use public restrooms without someone calling security. The college kids in the apartment upstairs urinated on her bedroom window. The world was actively discriminating against her. There is no favorite picture from these years. Jenny had forgotten how to smile. There was no question in my mind that something needed to change so Jenny could have space to navigate in the world.

Jenny was more than a tomboy. In fact, Jenny told me she was a boy, or at least, she wanted to be one. Or to say it more clearly, she was a boy, but nature (did I do this?!) didn't get it right. Isn't that every mother's fear? - that we would have children who did not have what they needed to survive? It was my fear, my struggle, my nightmare and my rebirth.

When I admitted these thoughts, I fell down the proverbial rabbit's hole. In 1995, my child was nineteen and struggling to go to school, work part-time and deal with the emotional impact of admitting to himself and me that he was a female-to-male transgendered person. I lost my dreams of what a daughter could be..

I was raised in a strong matriarchal family and am proud of being a woman. There was a sense of betrayal - my daughter didn't want to be my daughter. We shared a middle name with my mother. I would never have biological grandchildren to share that tradition. What would happen to the table that had been passed down from oldest daughter to oldest daughter for seven generations? What would I do with childhood pictures? How could I reconcile Jenny and the soon-to-be Daniel as being the same person? What about pronouns? My first reaction was "NO - this is NOT going to happen - not in my lifetime!" I wouldn't even discuss the issue.

Fortunately for us, Daniel stepped back and gave me time to think. After mulling the issue over, my biggest fear was that being transgendered meant that my child would never have a life with a partner, children, and a successful career. Fortunately, I had the opportunity of attending a national Female-to-Male conference held in Seattle. Most of the people I met there were established with careers and relationships. I started to believe there was a future for my child. I loved my child but still couldn't imagine what the end of this journey would look like or how I would manage it. One sensitive man from British Columbia sensed my confusion; he came up to me and assured me that he had been watching my child and was sure he would make a successful transition to being a man.

14

At 20, Daniel dropped out of college and lived in the world for a year as a man. His counseling had been successfully completed. The next stage became the central point of my hardest struggle- because my child was so young I felt that my help was actively needed to help provide the much needed new chance at life. I had asked him not to start his physical changes until he was 21. The time Daniel gave me by respecting my request was what I needed to intellectually accept the physical changes that were going to happen. At 21, he started taking hormones. In December 1997, I took Daniel to the hospital for his surgery and was in the recovery room with him.

I learned the details of hormones and cleaned the surgery incisions. I noticed the pimples as his beard came in and rubbed his muscles when they cramped from growing. I shared the additional expenses as he outgrew his clothes and boots and had to replace them. There was no place to hide and no way to escape.

I lost my ease in dealing with society. Preparations for my oldest son, Aaron's, wedding were agonizing. People who knew only Jenny had to be told about Daniel. We had to deal with their father's anger and frustrations, "can't he be a girl this one time?" Aaron, a biological male, identified potential trouble makers and recruited his friends to be ready to evict guests if they mistreated Daniel. My daughter-in-law spent hours on the seating plan to try to keep Daniel and myself buffered by safe people.

I lost part of my family. One of my brothers and his wife no longer let me be alone with my niece because of the "freak" I raised. Other family members just disappeared when we said "you have to call Daniel, Daniel, and treat him with respect."

I lost my sense of self. I discovered prejudice and hypocrisy that I didn't know existed within me. I thought a good parent was totally accepting all the time. I didn't like discovering I had selfish parts that didn't want what was best for my child. There was incredible anger towards Daniel: "I have to deal with this or that situation because of you." I didn't want to give up my dream daughter. I didn't want to learn that gender has a wide range of expressions and is more than

15

male and female. There was guilt that threatened to immobilize me.

Over time, Daniel connected with successful transgendered men who became mentors. They helped educate him on legal and "passing" issues and the search for the right doctors. Spencer Bergstedt and Jason Cromwell showed Daniel ways to be a man without being a biological male. Aaron took over the role of teaching Daniel what he needed to know from the perspective of a biological male.

In addition, I have found a partner who knows Daniel is transgendered but has never known him as Jenny. Seeing my son through her eyes and the eyes of her children reinforces the understanding that Daniel's decision to start this process early in his life was the right one. The ability that Jean, my partner, has given me to see Daniel as an integrated person plus the space our male friends and Aaron have unknowingly created have allowed me to deal with the emotional impact of all these changes.

Because Daniel was so young, I got to see the changes on an every-day basis and was able to witness the incredible joy the changes were bringing him. I believe that the transition has been easier for both of us than if he had been an adult child because Daniel never lived in the world as a woman — there was not much to unlearn. This has become the central point of some of my greatest joys.

What are the results of this journey? I gained an incredible, sensitive and caring son who is comfortable with himself. (The down side is that we can't go out in public without someone flirting with him.)

There is great growth in knowing that gender is fluid and people can decide for themselves what traits they want to include as part of their most intimate self. If my partner were to die, I would probably search for a transgendered person because the ones I've met have internalized the parts of female and male that I most respect in individuals.

Freedom. Daniel and I can go out in public easily now. It used to be that we could go out to dinner or the movies but never both together because Daniel couldn't use public restrooms. Last month we went out to a movie and dinner the same evening for the first time in more than five years.

As I integrate the pain and grief of my losses into the new person I'm becoming, I have a stronger sense of myself and my own worth. I see discrimination that has always existed but that I was too insulated to recognize. I'm Co-chair of the Cultural Diversity Committee at work because I have found a way and place to effect a change.

I have gained a new respect for my older son, his wife and my parents because they have completely accepted Daniel. My partner and her daughters have helped create a safe home where every one can be who they were meant to be.

We laugh. Aaron, a computer person, tells people his brother's "software was installed in the wrong hard drive" and is finally being put in the right box. I tell people my son had surgery for a birth defect that couldn't be corrected until he was an adult. The family snickers every time I repeat this to "outsiders." My mother, who has Alzheimer's, called Jenny "Daniel," the name of her deceased brother for several years before Daniel started talking about being a man. She recently told her doctor that there was nothing wrong with her mind. After all, she knew before anyone that Daniel was just like her brother.

There is a sense of peace now because of the love which is expressed in many different ways. Daniel never corrects his grandmother when she says Jenny because he knows she meant to say "Daniel" but the circuits got crossed. Daniel is patient in educating me and letting me ask questions. We count new facial hairs and are delighted with the heavy hair on his stomach and legs. This year for the first time, he can go swimming. He's comfortable with his body and has swimming trunks Jean gave him to celebrate his chest surgery. Dan calls his brother to ask, "Can I punch out the guy who cuts me off in traffic?," "What do I do with a tuxedo handkerchief?," "Can I sit down in the men's rest room?" He has started getting calls from women who want to go out with him, and yes, they know he's transgendered.

And what of the questions I had when I gained a son? I found the answers. Daniel modified his middle name from Elaine to Lain. He will still inherit the table - he was the oldest daughter. Learning that gender bends and is flexible has helped re-define what really matters in a person. I have gained the ability to use the right pronoun when I'm talking about past, present and future events. I can get angry with the situation and not blame the person. I hope that science eventually finds a way to identify this as a birth defect so people starting the process can have financial assistance while transitioning.

I lost the dreams of a daughter but have gained dreams of a son. And I have discovered that I will always be a mother — the dreams are for me alone. Do you think maybe Daniel will find a nice woman with a little girl I can spoil and love? There is a new favorite picture. Daniel is wearing a black tuxedo with a forest green vest. His white shirt shows how dark his hair and eyes are. He is laughing happily.

Like Alice in Wonderland, I have learned no matter how things change they also remain the same. You have to start a journey before it can end.

~~~~~~~~~~

The daycare teacher didn't know about our family's history, but looking at the two of them, she had no doubt Kai was Marcelle's child: "You couldn't deny that child if you wanted to," she told Marcelle one day. "He looks like you birthed him yourself!"

The funny thing is, he did! (Loree Cook Daniel)

MY "KEWL" KID
Catherine Dale*

I am a former elementary school teacher, raising two pre-teens, Linda* and James*, mostly alone. We all enjoy the Colorado outdoors: camping, hiking, skiing, as well as a love of reading and mountain gardening. We have worked out an in-home style so James can occasionally express his unshakable belief he is a really a girl.

My younger child, James, is special, but it has taken me some time both to accept him as he is and to learn how to deal with him. He wants to be a girl.

James first showed a preference for his sister's old toys when he was still a toddler, barely walking. My husband and I (I was still married then) assumed he was drawn to the colors; her toys were often more colorful, brighter, more interesting to the eye. Later, when he was walking and interacting with other children his age, I would overhear him (or be told by another child's mother) that he was announcing to all who would listen that he WAS really a girl but that he needed "medicine" or needed to "get better" before he would look like a girl. All this was going on about the time I was going through the divorce. Although not much was amusing during those days, my husband and I still smiled at James's fantasy. He was so serious about it all.

His interest in his sister's toys continued. I remember the day I sat him down and told him boys shouldn't play with dolls and nail salon kits. He said to me something like "Why, what's so wrong with girls?" Not "what's so wrong with girls' STUFF" but "what's

19

so wrong with GIRLS"! I knew right then and there that if I didn't lighten up, he'd start believing that girls were somehow lesser human beings and that their STUFF was in some way shame-connected. I was speechless.

Talk about Instant Enlightenment! I did a complete about-face and told him that there was nothing wrong with his wanting to "be a girl" once in a while, in the safety of our home. He has never pushed the limits.

He is so much happier when I give him as much latitude as he wants, within reason. When he does "dress up," it's with his sister, Linda's, permission (because he does use her things). She thinks it's "kewl." Our most daring adventure (and the only time he's asked to go outside of our home) was when I allowed him to tag along to Safeway wearing his sister's floral parka and with barrettes in his hair. He didn't act-up or anything, just clung to my hand as we went up and down the aisles. Linda, on the other hand, seems perfectly content in her "skin" — at least, within normal limits for a pre-teen girl!

James has never really backed off his insistence that he IS a girl. It's not that he wants to play "dress up" in order to look LIKE a girl. He acts genuinely confused at times because I'm reluctant to buy him outfits like those his little playmates wear. He often asks "Am I pretty?" or says "I want to be beautiful." This amuses my older child, Linda, who'll muss James' hair and say something like "Oh you are the prettiest girl, next to me!" To which James will just smile, or shoot back, "No, I am the prettiest!" And so it goes.

So, all in all, he's a much happier kid these days. Where it all will lead... who can tell? But I refuse to get all angst-up (my new term) before I have to!

A TRANSSEXUAL IN TEHERAN
Zari Ghasemi*

I was born in Teheran, Iran in 1947 into a well-educated middle-class family with four siblings. I earned a Bachelor's degree in Business Administration and married a college classmate. We then went to England to continue our education. While there, I gave birth to our first son in 1970. We returned to Iran in 1974 and in 1978 our second son, Noosheen, was born.

In 1979 the Islamic fundamentalist Revolution seized control of Iran. It was in Iran in the early years after the Revolution that our son, Noosheen, grew up. While we had no idea what to think, we knew from the beginning that his behavior was totally different from our older son's; he liked to play with my dresses, shoes and other clothes. When Noosheen was four I took him to a psychiatrist recommended by his kindergarten staff. The doctor advised us not to show any reaction to what he did. I began to grow concerned about his effeminacy because, in our environment, differences were not tolerated. Noosheen's strength seemed to be his early ability to communicate clearly, which our friends all thought was quite sweet and fascinating.

As Noosheen started school we remained concerned about him, but I realize now that we were not really seeing everything; he was learning to hide some of his more unacceptable behavior in reaction to our scoldings. Occasionally, however, when I caught him I kept saying to myself that he would grow out of it, without really facing up to what it was. As time passed and issues became more serious, our friends started advising me to consult specialists. I saw a psychiatrist who said Noosheen was effeminate because he identified

21

too closely with me. He advised us to have him spend more time with my husband and his adult male friends.. We wanted to do whatever we could to ensure that he would grow up healthy and "normal." We were afraid he might develop into an outcast; his life could even be in danger.

Nothing seemed to work. We simply could not change Noosheen's ways. By the time he was about eleven years old, he had grown very withdrawn. He never played with the boys in the neighborhood and, at this age, the neighborhood girls did not like to play with him as much as before. At this age, children were invariably separated by gender. It was actually considered to be a violation of norms and social standards for a boy to be around girls much at this age. We were concerned about Noosheen's present and future. Stigma attached to us and to him for being different. Even our immediate family was making derogatory remarks. (In retrospect, everyone was avoiding saying the most obvious fact, which was that even at this young age Noosheen was showing signs that he was homosexual, the only thing anybody could think of.)

In Iran, families are very close and their judgment is very important. Isolation from the extended family could be detrimental to one's status in the society and can leave an individual vulnerable. The community in general is closed and very judgmental. For example, any deviation from the required standards of clothing set by the authorities brings trouble.

By his teenage years, Noosheen was more and more withdrawn. I realize now that he was terrified to tell us what was happening to him. Although my husband and I like to consider ourselves relatively well-educated and liberal, it is hard for us to deny that we, too, were affected by the sharply intolerant society we lived in, even becoming reluctant to take Noosheen out with us. Only two years ago did Noosheen finally confide in me the extent to which he had been brutally mistreated. He told me how he had been constantly ridiculed, assaulted, pushed down and beaten in the stomach by his classmates while others just watched.

Now even finding the right school for Noosheen was a problem because they screened students, not only on the basis of academic merit, but also on their beliefs, conformity to the set standards in terms of clothing, behavior, etc. Noosheen was not an irresponsible or disruptive student by any standard, but he did not conform to the mainstream of that society and that put him at a great disadvantage. We started getting warnings that he should not mix with students older than himself. (All schools in Iran are single sex only; there are no co-educational institutions).

Noosheen was an intelligent student with an excellent academic record, and we were prepared to pay higher tuition to get him into a better, stricter school, which we hoped would "cure" his problems. We both had respectable jobs and we succeeded in finding a relatively good school that could guarantee to some extent that Noosheen had a place in a university in Iran. This was very important because achieving entry into an Iranian university is not easy.

While attending this new school, Noosheen's situation deteriorated. The school was extremely intolerant of his non-conformity. Noosheen started experiencing depression, crying without any reason, becoming withdrawn and fearful. He was also in love with one of his male classmates. Again it was only much later that he told me about how much pressure he had experienced during this time, how his classmates still ridiculed him.

It was the last year of high school when Noosheen became extremely depressed and unhappy. We again took him to a doctor, a specialist in teenage sexual problems. It was only after six months that he diagnosed Noosheen as a transsexual. At this time our son would not talk to my husband or me or any of his friends. He would draw the curtains in his room, remain isolated and cry hysterically. Even then we thought of it as homosexuality, the only condition we understood. Noosheen was even arrested twice by the police because of the same thing— that his behavior was that of a homosexual. Transsexuality is hardly known in that society.

In the meantime, Noosheen attempted suicide as a way out. During a six-month period he attempted suicide ten times. He cut his wrist, and his arm (with a knife mostly and in one occasion with a razor blade). He used sleeping tablets, and once he tried all the medicine in the medicine cabinet. Each attempt occasioned a trip to the hospital. As we realized that Noosheen was desperately trying to find a way out of his unbearable life, we became more sympathetic and supportive. I was devastated and could not think of any way out of the misery all three of us were in.

I had been let go of one good job shortly after the Revolution for non-conforming and later worked as an English teacher. By the summer before Noosheen's last year of high school, I had been working in a very demanding job. As Noosheen was going through these intense difficulties, and needed a great deal of attention I decided to seek leave from work. Because I could not explain any part of the reason for this I eventually lost a very rare, good job. But I could not risk Noosheen's life to stay at work.

Meanwhile Noosheen was extremely fearful of leaving the house and refused to go to school; even private evening classes did not work out. We knew by this time that the only way to survive was to find a way to take him out of the country. Anytime he went out he could be arrested. His future safety as well as his possibilities of advancing in Iranian society (education, employment) depended on maintaining a clean record.

My husband managed to get Noosheen exempted from the military service. Then, after a long struggle with the British Embassy in Tehran, we took him to England, but his presence there made our older son very uncomfortable. I decided then to leave for the United States. Before my six-month stay in England was over I made an appointment with the American Embassy in London, where I applied for and was granted a visitors' visa.

I came to the USA in October 1996 and in June 1997 Noosheen entered the USA to join me. My husband had flown with him to the U.S. Embassy in Vienna to obtain a special visa, as my minor child.

Right now our life is extremely difficult as few employers are prepared to sponsor me. I am, therefore, unable to work and as a result our financial situation is critical, jeopardizing Noosheen's education and future treatment. I am VERY MUCH willing to stay here, provided I can obtain a Green Card and can support myself and Noosheen. Here I have found support groups and parents who are dealing with the same issues as I am; there is tolerance and the society is much less judgmental. This is so very important because my new daughter, who is at the early stages of transition, needs acceptance badly. Noosheen has been on hormones since January '98 and dresses androgynously now. Her professors and classmates are tolerant and the ones who know about her are very accepting.

My husband still works in Iran and is supporting us. If I succeed in obtaining a Green Card and find a job here we would definitely immigrate. For now I feel that I should be with Noosheen to do everything I can to let her settle in a new country and transition more comfortably.

Also I feel this stage is like the birth of a new child and I do not want to miss that. So I am staying by her.

YOU NEVER HAD A DAUGHTER
by Susan Bennett

I have a background in journalism and public relations, but have recently worked as a fundraiser, currently at a continuing care retirement community. This has given me a great respect for the wisdom of the elderly. Besides BC, I also have a 15-year-old son, who is quite pleased to have a big brother. I enjoy horseback riding, reading, gardening and water sports.

I see my experience raising a transsexual child in three stages: childhood, when gender preferences began to emerge but didn't seem to matter; early adolescence, when all of us were tormented but didn't know why; and now that we know, when we are finally able to make sense of the questions that have been forming in our minds for years and can help our child become the person he was meant to be.

From the start, Beecie was clearly different from the other little girls we knew. She preferred overalls over dresses. She liked her hair short, with no ribbons, bows or hairclips. She was fascinated by male toy action figures, especially those that came equipped with weapons. She wore superman pajamas at night, an astronaut costume at Halloween, and a Fisher Price tool belt on Saturdays as she followed her father around the house.

During this stage, Beecie's differences didn't seem to matter — to her or anyone else. She was simply a tomboy — a girl who refused to let herself be defined by society's expectations. It was incredibly "politically correct" at the time, and I was proud of myself for being the consummate '80s mom.

Yet at times, I wondered about my child. On Beecie's third birthday, I laid out an outfit of shorts and a matching shirt with ruffles. BC (the name my child uses today) says this day is one of his most vivid childhood memories. He recalls begging me to let him wear something else, to no avail. I vaguely recall asking Beecie why she didn't like the outfit, and being confused by her unhappy answer: "I want to be a boy."

Beecie got off to a solid start in school. But when it came time for report cards, her kindergarten teacher had one curious comment. "Beecie plays roughly with the puppets. She makes them fight with one another." The comment didn't surprise me. But it did make me realize how "male" Beecie's behavior seemed to others. I am certain the teacher would not have made the comment had Beecie been a genetic boy.

In first grade, Beecie refused to take off her sweater after recess one day even though she was hot and flushed from playing outdoors. The teacher was so concerned, she sent Beecie to the counselor for a talk. When the counselor probed, she learned the reason for Beecie's stubbornness: the front of her shirt had a huge pink appliquéd flower on it, and Beecie did not want anyone to see it.

After the pink shirt incident, I tried to be more sensitive to Beecie's clothing preferences. She hated to shop, but when she did agree to go, she headed straight to the boys' department. I winced every time, and dreamt of the day my daughter and I would enjoy real shopping trips together.

Beecie's third grade school picture is one of my favorites. She is wearing an outfit her grandmother sent, a gray cotton jumper printed with tiny pink flowers and a white blouse with a ruffled collar. It was not her usual school attire, and I have no idea how I got her to wear it that day. But there she is, her sweet, freckled face smiling into the camera, the picture of a perfect, happy little girl. As she grew older, I began to realize what an aberration that picture was. And yet, I still look at it sometimes and wonder where that little girl went.

When Beecie was in fourth grade, she made a valiant attempt to be like the other girls. The New Kids on the Block were the rage, and

Beecie wore New Kids T-shirts, bought New Kids tapes, plastered New Kids posters on her bedroom wall, and swooned over Donnie with the best of them. Later, she would tell me that she never liked the New Kids, and was just trying like mad to fit in.

Then, Beecie got a skater hair cut – parted to the side, short on one side, longer on the other and shaved up the back. It was definitely a boy cut, and she was proud of it.

All through primary school, the other kids had taken Beecie's individuality in stride. She had always been different, and they seemed to accept her without question. In fifth grade, that changed when she attended a new school. One night, I came into her room to find her lying on her bed, face to the wall. When I asked her what was wrong, she began to cry –- something she almost never did. At lunch that day, she had been rejected by a group of girls when she tried to sit with them. "Who asked you?!" they had demanded cruelly.

Another night, Beecie came into the kitchen while I was preparing dinner and told me her chest hurt. We ruled out P.E. class as a cause, since the current sport was soccer. Finally, I asked her to show me where it hurt. She put her hands to her breasts, where two small knots were beginning to form. "Beecie," I said, "those are your breasts!" Her face fell, and she looked grief-stricken. Later, she told me that as a child, she would stand naked in front of the mirror and look at her chest, dreading the day that she would have breasts.

During her middle school years, Beecie grew progressively sullen, angry, and belligerent. She had always been an intense, strong-willed child whose personality tended to dominate the household. But now she began to lash out, screaming at her stepfather, beat up unmercifully on her younger brother, and challenge me physically, once blocking me from entering our home. She was obviously very unhappy, but I didn't know how to help her. I offered to take her to a therapist, but she refused. Once or twice, she broke down and cried, saying she felt "all wrong" but didn't know what to do about it.

I knew adolescent girls were supposed to be moody and emotional, so I tried to believe it was just hormones. But deep inside, I worried, and with good cause. Later, BC would tell me that he was so tormented by ninth grade, he probably would have taken his life had it not been for his friend Christine, to whom he was able to express the growing fear that he was a freak.

It was during that year, BC later told me, that he knew for certain he was a male inside, but he was frightened and confused by the disparity between his body and his brain. He thought he was crazy and alone, the only person who had ever felt that way. In agony, he became severely depressed. It was only his nightly phone conversations with Christine that got him through.

Finally, to his great relief, BC learned that there was a name for the way he felt. On the Internet one night, he discovered the term "transsexual," and he knew there were others like him.

It was another six months before the "T-word" came into my life. Still worried about my child, I began to snoop in his room for some clue of what was wrong. One day, I came across a spiral notebook which he was using as a journal. There were writings about being a man, and across one page were the words, "I am a transsexual." I was horrified — so much so that I kept this revelation to myself as I tried to make sense of what I had read.

Around this time, BC began to diet and exercise excessively, and then showed signs of mild bulimia. It was time to seek professional help, and this time BC accepted my offer. I was on the phone interviewing a prospective therapist, when BC picked up another receiver and heard me say, "My daughter thinks she is a transsexual." I had never confronted him with my journal discovery, but now he came to me and said, "Mom, we have to talk."

BC and I sat up for hours that night. He described the growing awareness of being male throughout his life. He told me how tormented he had been in middle school, how hard he had tried to fit in, how terrifying it had been to feel so different and to not understand why. He told me how, finally, he had confessed his fears to Christine and how she had listened and comforted him, a true friend. He told me about desperately searching on the Internet for clues to what he was experiencing, and finally discovering that it had a name and that he was not alone.

As I listened, I felt totally inadequate as a mother for not, somehow, knowing how very precarious my child's emotional state had been. My heart wrenched at the terrible pain he described, and I silently thanked God for sending Christine to share his burden when I couldn't. BC apologized for not telling me earlier. He said he wanted to, but he feared that I would be upset. "Well," I responded, "it is hard for me to comprehend all of this. I feel like I'm losing my daughter." To that, BC responded with a remark that I will never forget: "But Mom," he said calmly, "you never had a daughter."

When I thought about it, I knew he was right, and this realization has been my saving grace. For when I got over being horrified long enough to stop and think, I knew that what I was hearing made absolute perfect sense, given all that that had gone before during my child's life. It was as if I was finally getting an answer to the question that had been forming in my mind for years.

After several false starts, we found a wonderful psychiatrist who had been associated for years with a gender identity program at a nearby university. At our first visit, I put up a brave front, but he could apparently see the difficulty I was having accepting the situation. I will always be grateful to him for giving me something positive to hold onto at that moment. After listening to BC for a few minutes, he commented on the tremendous inner strength which BC seemed to possess. Then he turned to me and said, "You must be some kind of parent, because that's where this kind of inner resource comes from in a child."

After a series of visits, he confirmed that BC showed all the classic signs of transsexualism. Since then, BC has seen him regularly, and he has been a kind, thoughtful and wise advisor and sounding board, supporting BC through his final two years of high school. Although semi-retired, he has promised to be available as long as BC needs him.

During the last two years, BC has moved forward with growing courage and anticipation towards becoming the person he was meant to be. During this period, he came out slowly to selected friends, co-workers, teachers and school administrators. Every single time, he has been met with kindness, interest and support. He started hormone injections during the spring of his senior year. At graduation, he wore men's clothing under his robe.

In his opening remarks at graduation, the principal said there were many things for which he would remember the class of '98. Then he began to name students that he would especially remember and why. To my complete surprise, the first name to come out of his mouth was my child's: "I will remember BC Phillips and Lisa — for their courage," he said to an audience of several thousand.

With that one remark, the principal gave BC and me both a precious gift. By acknowledging BC's courage, the principal took my child's greatest struggle and granted to it a sense of dignity and respect that I will remember and appreciate for the rest of my life.

~~~~~~~~~~

I am a transgender warrior, devoting my life to fighting a culture that seeks to dispose of me by any means necessary. This is my existence - my life - my destiny. There are not enough tears....

(Jessica Xavier)

~~~~~~~~~~

I've been mistaken for my wife too! I mean, the old me is my husband! I mean, I uh, oh, I don't know, you know! It's so confusing, like the song "I'm My Own Grandpa"

This has happened numerous times, but the one I remember best is changing my name at the Incredible Universe, an electronics store which uses membership cards. I went in and handed a young woman my card and told her I needed to change my name. She scanned the card, looked at her screen, and got that confused look on her face. She handed back the card and said, "This isn't your card. It's your husband's card." I said, "No, this is my card. I'm not married, I need to change my name. I need to change my first name to Tamara and my middle initial to K. She took the card back, scanned it, handed it back and said, "No, this isn't your card!" After several exchanges like this she finally scanned me really close and got very puzzled. I finally got it across to her that it was my card, not my husbands. She changed the name and I thanked her. As I walked away from her still puzzled look, her eyes wide open, she turned to another woman behind the counter and began to talk girl talk (you know, that secret, half whispered, shoulder's hunched talk that we women do), very excitedly. I'll never forget it! (Tammy Fisher)

~~~~~~~~~~

An old phrase takes on a new meaning - I like to tell people I'm a self-made woman. (Roselyn Lisle)

PART II

LEARNING FROM OUR CHILDREN
OF ALL AGES

FROM ANGER TO ACCEPTANCE - A MOTHER' STORY
Barbara Lister

I was born in 1913 in Boston, a beginning which shaped my standards and values. After graduation from Wellesley College I married James M. Lister, Urban Planner, and had five wonderful children. Later I began teaching adult literacy classes, have continued tutoring, and get my greatest satisfaction as a teacher.

My son has become my daughter, and I have recently returned from accompanying him/her to surgery, the final step in the gender-transformation from Michael to Miquelle. How did I feel when my eldest son — Swarthmore, Peace Corps, committed Christian — announced to me that he felt unsuited to being a man and wished to enter the world of make-up and panty hose and live as a woman? How do I feel, three years later, when the gender change has been completed? This is the story of my journey from shocked outrage to acceptance.

Nothing in Michael's life had prepared me for such a revelation. He was the oldest son in our "normal" suburban family. My husband and I assumed that our five would grow up happy and well-adjusted in their busy life of school and Scouts, horses, and family togetherness. Michael was a rosy-checked, energetic toddler, a husky boyish youngster. The only intimation to me of any difficulty came when, at the age of age seven, after the birth of his twin sisters, he began to complain of stomach aches that enabled his to stay home from school. When our pediatrician could find no physical cause, I chalked it up to sibling rivalry. Michael did tell me that he was frightened by the death of a boy in his class and of a favorite teacher; privately he resolved to be "good" lest he die, too. Perhaps that was the reason for his becoming a more anxious and uncertain boy. Or, perhaps, was this the first stirring of what Michael has described to me later as a feeling that his inner self did not match the body he had been given? In the happy commotion of a big family I was not really aware of what he was feeling. Even today, Miquelle, with the help of a psychiatrist, trying to piece together the past, cannot be sure what was going on in his troubled child's mind to bring such a change.

As an adolescent, Michael studied dutifully and was valedictorian of his class. He tried out unsuccessfully for the basketball and football teams, but developed into a skillful bird-watcher. I recognized that he was shy and awkward around girls, but because I had suffered from a similar anxiety in the world of high school dating I thought it uncomfortable but natural. At Swarthmore he majored in Chemistry but had little interest in life in a lab. The opportunity to be a Peace Corps teacher in Malaysia was a peak experience. He liked his teaching at an English speaking boys' school, made good friends of both sexes, and savored the exotic sights and tastes and cultural diversity that is Malaysia.

His re-entry into ordinary living was to him, as to many Peace Corps volunteers, a traumatic experience. Thinking to continue his success, he became a teacher in an inner- city, racially-mixed school in New Haven. No longer did the pupils rise as he came into the room and politely chorus "Good morning, Mr. Lister." Instead, he experienced the panic known only by a teacher who feels completely out of control of the class in front of him. One night a midnight call came to us from Michael, "Can you help me? I'm afraid I'll jump out of the window." The resulting depression was gradually alleviated by the healing care of a residential treatment program. Michael subsequently managed to weather a good many years in steady but unfulfilling jobs and a marriage that ended in divorce. Through it all he was aided by his Christian beliefs which nourished him but added to his sense of guilt as he faced a scary Father God. Always to the outside world he was the dependable Michael, loved by his family and friends because he was kind and good.

36

About six years ago, a second hospitalization for depression led him to move to Cleveland to stay with me, recently widowed. He found a new job in a travel agency. I felt that finally he was gaining confidence and new skills. However, my optimism was shattered on the fateful morning which ushered in a new relationship between him and the outside world. On that morning he showed me a newspaper article about a successful Cleveland entertainer who had changed gender from man to woman. While I was scanning the article with slight interest, he plucked up his courage to say, "I showed you this because I want to become a woman." My reaction was predictable. I vaguely remembered a sensational Christine Jorgenson and a Renee Richards who had been barred from a woman's tennis tournament because she had been a man. But I never watch Oprah Winfrey, and the description "drag queen" was not in my vocabulary.

I was horrified, that this 50-year-old son, slightly balding, conscientious, caring, could contemplate an action so bizarre and repugnant. Several days later, when I had cooled down somewhat, he gingerly suggested that I might want to meet someone who had made the change, perhaps invite that person to dinner so that we could talk. My answer, I am ashamed to say, was, "I don't think I could have such a person under my roof." We finally compromised and agreed to meet at a restaurant. "Chris" was waiting for us, well-dressed, feminine enough, self assured. During the dinner conversation, which was polite though a bit strained, I learned that she had a successful freelance advertising business, and that her mother, at that time, lived in the same expensive retirement community as many of my friends. I accepted her suggestion that I call her mother. Here, I realized, would be another mother like myself who could talk to me about her pain as she had watched a cherished son make a change in gender. Talking with Mrs. H. made me feel less isolated and frightened. She had seen a depressed and unhappy son become a happy and coping new person. She assured me that a mother's acceptance is possible.

Still I poured out to my journal a tumult of feelings, usually accompanied by tears. Anger—why was he doing this to me? Fear—

would he lose his job and have no future? Embarrassment — how could I ever be seen in his company? I remember crying out bitterly to my journal, "I want to have a temper tantrum right in front of him so he will know what he is doing to me!"

I faced a dilemma. Having Michael live with me was a pleasant arrangement. I liked to cook a meal for someone to come home to. Most importantly, his being there to help made it possible for me to remain in my home. I faced a bleak choice: either adapt to Michael's gender change or move into a retirement community.

At this point I had some help on the road to acceptance. I hesitantly confided in a kindly woman minister who said to me, "You love Michael, don't you? Then you have no choice." I joined a Grief Group at my church because, even though my grief was not due to a death, I still keenly felt the loss of a loved one. In the group I could pour out my mixture of anger and grief and be listened to with compassion. I also found help from Cleveland's well-established "Gender Program," enabling me to talk with a psychiatrist in Michael's presence.

His brothers and sisters were also struggling. One daughter joined Michael and me for a week-end at a retreat house where our sharing and the silence of the place brought us some measure of peace. But the confrontation of the siblings at Christmas time was bitter and largely unforgiving. Over the months each gradually at his own pace accommodated to the change. However, it was not until a family reunion after the surgery that the structure of the family re-formed to include this new person whom they decided to christen with a more affectionate name, "Kelly."

Meanwhile, Michael, who had always tried to please, was bucking his family and society's expectations by going through the steps necessary to become Miquelle. With the help of thrift shops he began to assemble a woman's wardrobe for the office. A friend who sold Avon products helped him with makeup. I went with him, embarrassed, of course, to choose a becoming wig. He tried dressing where he would not be recognized and also at the meetings of transsexuals and "cross dressers" (to me, ugly terms), who got together once a month for support and information. He had regular counseling under the Gender Program, and also embarked on the long, expensive process of electrolysis.

Another step involved writing all the members of the extended family, trying to explain to them that he was becoming the person he had always thought himself to be. Then there were the legal steps — driver's license, bank account, Social Security, passport. The final hurdle was the job. Much to my amazement, the office, because his work did not require him to meet the public, gave him permission to work there as Miquelle. I watched in anguish as the new person set off to meet the test. How did she look? If you were critical you would focus on the man's hands, the size 13 shoes, the masculine bones of the face. If you loved her, you would focus on the graceful clothes, the hair style and make-up that softened the face, the new radiance to the eyes. So I could pray that — perhaps, possibly — she would not be too conspicuous.

For two years the counseling program continued. In a new church, Miquelle was accepted along with her story. She began to develop a style in dressing; shopping, especially in those surprise-filled thrift shops, was a hobby we both discovered. In spite of my lingering embarrassment, she came eventually to functions at my church where my friends greeted her courteously as I self-consciously introduced her as my daughter. One of my hardest lessons was to use the pronoun "she."

In a significant step forward for her, when her job was phased out because of a merger, she was able to get a more responsible job in another travel agency where the workers knew her story but were ready to welcome her. Friends, new or loyal old friends, seemed to extend to her a deeper level of caring. A new personality was emerging — more affectionate, more self-assured, and certainly happier. She felt ready for surgery, but permission had to be given by the Gender Board. Under their strict supervision and with continued professional counseling, Miquelle had begun taking female hormones after having lived for a year as a woman. Now she was judged ready to make an appointment for the surgery with a skillful plastic surgeon in Montreal. I decided to go with her for the first few days of hospitalization.

Being with her during that time made a profound impression on me. I learned that every week a new group of patients came from all over the country, even fundamentalist Christians, for sexual reassignment. Miquelle was not unique. I heard stories of pain and rejection. A surprising uniformity was in their reports. Most of them agreed that, when they were about five, when school began to separate girls and boys, each began to have the shameful certainty that he could not feel as other boys did. It was a guilty feeling which he dared not share with anyone. As he grew older he tried to hide it by "macho" acts like growing a beard. Perhaps he married and fathered children, hoping that the feelings would go away. Still he felt, as they all described it, like a woman "trapped in a man's body." The struggle to deny this feeling led usually to depression, often even to thoughts of suicide. I heard, too, of the joy of the new identity. One newly-emerged woman who had just opened a bank account in her new name exulted, "Now I can accept myself! Now I can love myself! Now I am who I am!" Listening, I began to accept with my heart as well as my head, what I had previously resisted believing — that this phenomenon of gender mismatching is genuine and compelling.

To accept these experiences as authentic I did not need the confirmation given to the skeptical by recent researchers in the Netherlands. In comparing a small region of the hypothalamus, where the roots of sexuality are thought to live, these researchers discovered a significant difference in the size of this tiny structure in the brain of male-to-female transsexuals as compared with normal males. The report concluded, "This finding may cast light on the larger issue of sexual identity, of what makes a person feel comfortable — or tormented — as a man or woman."

Miquelle says the structure of her brain makes little difference to her. What she does know, since the surgery, is that she feels herself to be wholly the person she was meant to be. As she said to me the other day, "Walking home tonight wearing a blouse and skirt, I realized a difference. I have worn skirts since 1993, but I still knew that part of my body was male. Now, though I still like to wear pretty clothes, I am no longer as concerned that my appearance be as feminine as possible so that no one will suspect my story. Now I feel real and genuine. I thank my Creator every day for allowing me to become a woman."

So now the transformation from Michael to Miquelle has reached a new plateau. I have changed too. When I began this parenting business I naively assumed that two competent parents plus a comfortable home environment would produce a series of "Dick and Jane" children who would go to the right colleges, get good jobs, and bring their children home for the holidays. My adult children, of course, have each had some difficult times in their lives, but the crises have been resolved and I could once more, on my Christmas cards, affectionately chronicle my children's doings. But Michael shattered my stereotype of what was acceptable behavior. I had to learn that loving involves letting go. The child you love must follow his own path no matter how unlike the one you would have chosen for him. I have had to grow into the realization that loving means accepting with compassion and without embarrassment. While learning this I have, it is true, lost a son but I have gained a daughter.

Post script — A Success Story

Two years later the memory of my anger has faded. as has the memory of that lost person, my eldest son, Michael. The new person, Kelly, has become familiar and loved. She wears her hair up in a knot to replace the more conspicuous wig. The hormones have rounded her figure and softened her face. To all but the most suspicious scrutiny she is just another tall, suitably dressed young woman. Her siblings, who still feel the loss of their brother, respond to the situation with varying degrees of' acceptance, but all now seem to have developed affection for the person she has become. There will always be awkward moments, as when a long-separated friend of mine asks, "And how is Michael?" or when, this summer, Kelly goes back for her Peace Corps reunion. In her job as travel agent she has gained respect for her competence; among those she meets she is valued for her friendliness, her thoughtfulness, and her willingness to reach out with empathy.

I have changed. too. As a token mother who is available to talk with any other troubled parents, I attend with Kelly a support group for Transsexuals, or Transgenders as they sometimes prefer to be called. In this group, numbering as many as forty from this geographical area, there are many variations in this process of gender change. Some have already gained security in their jobs or other relationships; others feel, as Kelly expressed it, 'like a tender little plant, pushing up so hopefully, but afraid that a cold wind will blow it over." It is still difficult for me to understand how the need for a gender transformation can be so compelling as to cause a person to risk rejection in her job, her church, and in some cases, the loss of spouse and children. I, however, have come to feel respect and affection for all those who, because of their feeling of incongruity, are willing to face so much pain in order, as they say, "to have their bodies match the selves they are within."

THE JOURNEY BEGINS
Karen and Bob Gross

Bob is from Cleveland, holds a Masters in Business and is a CPA. Karen and Bob have been married 35 years. Their other son is attending medical school. Karen, also from Cleveland, holds a BS in Education and taught school for several years before becoming the Office Manager for Bob's practice. Karen and Bob travel the midwest, speaking to college students and PFLAG chapters about TG/TS issues and what it is like to have a daughter who became a son.

Once upon a time I had a daughter. She had long, dark hair and beautiful eyes with long lashes. Her fingers were long and thin. Many people said they were the fingers of a piano player. At her birth my husband shouted, "It's a boy!" He was the only one near-by and loves to tease. Our daughter grew up to be our son, and he played the French horn. But let me start at the beginning of our journey.

I conceived after trying for almost 3 years. We were told to go to a drive-in movie, but settled on a visit to friends. We didn't know they were in the midst of a divorce and that we would have to sleep with their collie (his bed was the sleeper sofa) but that was when the journey began. Nine months later, Michelle was born.

The delivery was long and hard. Michelle didn't want to face the world. We spent two weeks in the hospital at a time when 4 days was normal. What happiness to go home with my daughter! Oh yes, I said that I wanted a girl so often that my mother thought I would leave a boy at the hospital! She was a gorgeous, good baby, and very bright. Everything was fine until I brought her brother home from the hospital when she was two.

Michelle went into the terrible two's and didn't come out of it for years. She was mostly a loner. By the age of six or seven, it was a struggle to get her to dress in any way feminine. Dresses and skirts were out; hair had to be short; playing with dolls was out of the question. She preferred her brother's underwear to her own. She insisted on shopping in the boys department. She was happiest in the company of boys (but not if the boy was her brother).

Michelle was very defensive and quick to retaliate to an inadvertent touch or well-meaning suggestion. She was depressed, although we never recognized it until later. She suffered from unexplained stomach aches. Her father blamed it on low self-esteem and had difficulty dealing with her negativity. We took her to psychologists, but Michelle wouldn't talk to them. (She told us recently that she was afraid of being called "crazy" if she us told what she really felt.) Through all of this she threw herself into schoolwork. She graduated with a degree in psychology, summa cum laude.

During college, Michelle met a wonderful, loving man and they married a year after graduation. We all hoped that marriage would make Michelle feel better about her self and resolve her problems. Michelle started a four year Law/Masters in Social Work program, and all was finally well... or so we thought.

Two years went by. Bob's dad was very ill. The kids came home for Thanksgiving and told us they were getting an annulment. They told us things were not working out and that they were just splitting up on a friendly basis. A few weeks later we found out why.

Michelle told us that she had been in counseling for several months, had finally faced her dilemma and decided to do something about it. Michelle was changing persona. He chose Mitchell as his new name. He had been in counseling for months with a gender specialist and would be starting hormones soon. We should expect to see physical changes such as lower voice and facial hair. Having completed most of his MSW work, and a year and a half of law school, he would now complete the second year of law school and do the last year as Mitchell.

Bob said it was a phase, but as a CPA with tax season approaching and his father's condition worsening, he tried his best not to think about it. Bob said, "It'll be all right. We will wake up in the morning and this will be a dream." I couldn't sleep. I cried all night.

The next day we remembered that we had seen a newspaper story about a male police officer who had changed to female. We called the station and she agreed to have lunch with us. Martha was a blessing. That meeting led to my attempts to seek out counseling and to find books on the subject. Before long I was educating the counselor and paying for the privilege. As the year went along, Bob was very supportive. He was accepting from the start, encouraging Mitch and defending him. They get along better now than at any time in the past.

Mitchell introduced me to e-mail and the Internet. Soon I had support and lots of information. I then reached out to try to find other parents of transsexual children. I found some in town and we began to meet together. And I found many new, supportive friends on the Internet. Bob and I worried about how our parents would take the news. They took it very well. After all, they all agreed, this was their grandchild, and they would support him as best they could.

What a difference in all of our lives! Mitch is finally a much happier person, with many new friends, a social life and a new life partner. He passed the bar examination, but really wants to work in the social services field. He moved back to town and now works in our accounting office. Mitch lived for a while with Bob's mother, who has been totally supportive of her grandson. We were supported by most of the people we told; those who didn't support us at first soon either adopted a different attitude or don't matter to us anymore.

A lot has happened with us in three years. Bob and I were introduced to PFLAG and now we travel, telling our story at PFLAG meetings. Our desire to support other parents of transsexual people has grown into a monthly meeting in our home, often with more than fifty people in attendance. Members of our group have been invited to speak on "T" issues at colleges, as far as 350 miles away.

"T" folks, their parents, spouses and former spouses, siblings, children, grandparents, and allies attend the meetings. Others in attendance have included MD's, PhD's, and clergy. We start with a potluck dinner, move to introductions, and then break into special interest groups. We respond to the many "thank you's" by suggesting that we are helped by being able to help. You do get what you give. We miss our daughter, but our son is a much happier person. We love him very much just the way he is.

Wedding Bells

Mitch is a female-to-male transsexual. Mitch's sexual orientation was, and is, toward males, so, while he presented as a woman, he was considered "straight," that is, attracted to men. Now that he presents as a man, his gender identity is male, but he is considered gay. (He tells us that he always self-identified as a gay guy in a woman's body.) Anyway, his sexual orientation didn't change when he transitioned. He changed his name and his driver's license, but not his birth certificate. In our state, it is considered a historical document and, by law, cannot be changed.

We used to kid Mitch that if he met a guy who could love him for who he was, he could make the front pages of the newspaper by having a same-sex marriage. He kidded us back, because he had already met a gay guy. They fell in love. CR knew of Mitch's journey, but it didn't matter to him. All he knew was that Mitch was the most wonderful person he had ever met and that he wanted to be with him for the rest of his life. The feeling was mutual between them. I might add that our whole family thinks that CR is the greatest, and is very happy for Mitch.

So, one day, Mitch and CR stopped at the courthouse to see if they could get a marriage license. They were sent to the magistrate who told them that our state didn't allow same-sex marriages and that the birth certificates had to be "one F and one M." Birth certificates were quickly produced that showed the requisite letters and the magistrate said, "Why didn't you say so in the first place?" A judge agreed that they could have a marriage license!

The next week, not wanting to wait for the judge to change his mind, a wedding was planned. CR and Mitch, Bob and I, and two members of the support group went to the courthouse. When we got into the courtroom, the judge, a different judge than the one that had approved the license, was visibly nervous. He examined the license, hesitated, and just when we expected him to refuse to do the marriage, said, "I have a standard ceremony. I use the words 'bride' and 'groom.' So as not to offend anyone, what do you want me to say?"

Mitch and CR quickly answered that he should use the word "spouse." The judge gave a grin and the ceremony began. When he got to the end, he said, "I now pronounce you (hesitation) MARRIED!" Mitch and CR talked to him afterward, and told the judge, who was very nice, what was happening. They reassured him that it only looked like he married two gay guys. We all shook hands and went out for lunch to celebrate the occasion.

The Butterfly

I now run a help line for the Transgender Special Outreach Network within PFLAG, a virtual support group. In one friend's words, we lost a daughter and gained a hobby! Mitch kids about starting a support group for children whose parents are more "out" than they are! Our latest project is starting a PFLAG chapter in our suburban area.

In today's society, some children are discarded for being transsexual. We discovered that most of our early fear, when Mitch came out to us, was self-directed. What would our parents say? Would we lose our friends? Will we ever be grandparents?

We found that it was our expectations for ourselves that were suffering. When we looked at our child, we soon realized that Mitchell had no choice but to be the person he really is. Our expectations had to take second place. We lost a daughter, but then we became parents of many children whose real parents, spouses, children, siblings, and friends wanted nothing more to do with them. Once upon a time there was a caterpillar...

~~~~~~~~~~

Holocaust survivor Elie Wiesel, in a poignant statement, remarked, "I swear never to be silent whenever and wherever human lives endure suffering and humiliation. We must always take sides. Neutrality helps the oppressor, never the victim. Silence encourages the tormentor, never the tormented. Sometimes we must interfere when human lives are endangered. When human dignity is in jeopardy, that place, at that moment, must become the center of the universe."

DALE
by Eileen Altrows

I am 61 and married to Jerry for 42 years. Jerry has recently retired and we enjoy being together. We have five grown children, ten grandchildren, and many pets. I love theatre, drawing, painting, needlepoint, calligraphy, walking, gardening, and traveling.

The sad little face. Hardly ever smiled. A good-natured, kind-hearted little girl. She grew. She became a teenager. The sadness still prevailed.

She was never happy with the way she looked. She didn't like her body. She would cover it up with very large T-shirts. She didn't like her breasts; she couldn't accept her body's development.

I couldn't understand why she felt the way she did. I used to tell her I thought she was good looking, but that didn't change things. She was always sad. It's hard to remember if I ever saw her smile at all.

She was insecure. Wanted to be with me all the time. She lacked self-confidence. I tried to build her self-confidence by pointing out her good qualities. No matter what I said or what I did, it didn't change. She was unsure of herself. She was afraid to talk to people.

She was more comfortable with boys. When she was young most of her friends were boys. I thought nothing of it at first until I realized she was mostly keeping the company of boys.

She was seventeen years old when my husband and I moved to British Columbia. Dale did not come with us. As we needed time to get settled, Dale and her sisters remained in Quebec. They stayed at our home with my parents, whom Dale loved very much. The pain of parting was mutual.

A few years went by. Dale told me she was having a breast reduction. I thought little about it After the surgery I thought Dale would feel more comfortable with her body. I was wrong.

Soon after the surgery Dale told me she had been dressing as a man for a few years. Somehow I wasn't shocked. One would have thought I'd be surprised. I don't know why I wasn't. I thought that if it made her happy, it was a good thing.

About one year after she told me she had been dressing as a man, I got a phone call from Dale. She told me she had something to tell me and that I'd best sit down to hear what she was going to say. Then she told me. She said, "Mother, I'm going to have a sex change." For a moment I was confused. I asked, "What did you say?" She repeated herself. I was shocked. I might have expected her to dress as a man but I never expected her to actually change into a man. I saw movies about this, and perhaps books, but I would never have expected this in my own family.

I remember Dale asking me at the time how I felt about it. I told her I was shocked and that I didn't know too much about the subject; that I would have to know more to become comfortable. I asked Dale several times if she would reconsider her decision. I tried presenting to her all the reasons why I thought it was possible to be happy as a female. No matter how hard I tried or how often I tried, nothing worked.

Yet, I love Dale very much and knew I would love her no matter what her gender was. The love I have for Dale is not only the love of a mother for her child, but the love for a person who is kind, warm and wonderful.

My main worry was the fact that my child would be having surgery, having her breasts totally removed. Just thinking of the pain she would go through tortured me. I could picture the pain that she would have. I could almost feel it.

Another kind of pain tortured me: the pain of knowing that Dale was so unhappy with her body as it was. This gender change was so important to her that she was willing to go through any amount of pain to make it happen.

50

All I wanted was for Dale to be happy. I wanted to see my child smile.

When Dale's voice started to change; he was so happy. I became happy with him. With new hair on his chest, his shoulders and chest becoming muscular, he was so happy and shared each new wonderful event with me. I was happy with him. When he was depressed due to hormonal therapy, I comforted him and gave him support.

When we visited and I saw Dale for the first time since the change, I looked at my child with the body of a young man ... a handsome young man ... a proud young man. I looked at him with admiration. I was proud to be his mother. He looked happy now!

He laughs now. He has fun now. He has confidence now.

I have lost a sad daughter. I have gained a happy son.

~~~~~~~~~~

"Those who say something cannot be done should not interupt those who are doing it."— Chinese proverb (Gary Bowen)

A LETTER TO ALLEN
by John Boenke

I am the father of a transsexual son. I am retired from an engineering management career and have long been active in civil rights issues I have been married for almost 44 years, have three wonderful children, and five beautiful grandchildren.

Dear Allen:

I have been meaning to write this letter for some time. It is long overdue, but I needed to get my thoughts in order so that I may say all I want to say in the best possible way.

I don't remember you ever being much trouble. Even when you were born, your timing was very helpful. I took Mom to the hospital with your brother, older by two years, riding along. We dropped Mom at the hospital and continued into town to pick up your Grandmother who was arriving at the bus station. She had agreed to come and help with the extra work necessitated by your arrival.

By the time I got back to the nursery, you had arrived and were there waiting for me, greeting me with a quiet or even, it might be called, a gracious smile. It was then I learned you were a little girl.

You were slow in learning to walk because of your infancy Celiac disease. Luckily, it was finally diagnosed, and we learned to control the illnes through a limited diet, until you grew out of it. You wanted to walk but did not quite have the strength or ability. So, as soon as I got home from work, you would come crawling over and want me to help you. You would hold my fingers, and we would go round and round in the halls. You led, toddling in front with arms raised, holding onto my fingers, and I walked along behind, bent over and carefully trying to avoid stepping on you as we gyrated along.

Then, again, your timing was excellent. One afternoon Mom and I were sitting on the floor, sending you back and forth between us. You would take one or two steps on your own, then collapse onto the floor or in our arms. Except once, you took a couple steps and kept going — and have been going ever since. That same evening your little sister arrived. It was almost as though you had known it was time for you to move on.

You were the artist in the family, you were the dreamy one, the quiet one, the one who took music a little more seriously than the others. You always did very well in school without making a big fuss about it. I remember you loved to play with your plastic toy horses. High school with your friends seemed to be a happy time for you. I remember how difficult it was for you to leave them when we moved to another city.

You were active in the local theater. I was really impressed how well you did in several roles. Remember "Wind in the Willows" and "The Seagull?" Then college. You were the last to leave. I recall your excitement, driving over to your college, and your joy in seeing your old high school friend from our previous city.

Then the bombshell! After your freshman year, you quietly let us know you considered yourself to be a lesbian. At first that was hard to take. We accepted what you said, but we did not talk about it. We went through the process which, we have since learned, many loving parents go through in the same situation. We first secretly denied it, thinking, "Oh, this is just a phase. Things will be different later." Then we felt guilty about it, "It must be our fault. What did we do wrong?" We worried about what kind of life you would have, but finally, over a period of years we came to accept your gayness.

Then, eighteen years later, just when your brother came down with leukemia and we were all struggling to deal with that, you dropped the other bombshell. You announced you might be a trans-sexual. At first I considered your timing was not very good on this one, but later I decided perhaps it was the best of all. While being concerned about your brother, we could not spend as much time worrying about you; and vice versa. It was a difficult time for us, but maybe the worrying time was cut in half while we did double duty!

Your announcement was hard to take, although by then we had had considerable experience comforting many other PFLAG parents. Working through our feelings and arriving at acceptance probably went a little quicker, but, still, all the stages of grief were there. We just recognized them more quickly.

We could understand your decision also. Your feelings did not match how you were living, and you had just not been aware of, nor considered, the alternatives before. Now there was more information and you understood yourself better then than ever before. Perhaps we should not have been so surprised. Looking back, I now realize there were some subtle hints earlier. In several of the stories you had written as a teenager, the main character was a man, written in first person, sometimes with a sexual theme. The way you prefered to dress was, undeniably, more male-oriented than female. Even in a recording of one of your concerts, when we played it again and finally "listened," you commented that, " I had always wanted to be a boy...." I'm sorry we did not hear you sooner!

So, just as your mother had previously taken the initiative in getting involved with PFLAG, she now jumped with both feet into the transsexual movement. The rest, as they say, "is history." Your Mom is very active in promoting the rights of all sexual minorities now, and I support that completely. I tag along to do what I can. She says it is useful that I am there, even if I'm often not sure, myself.

Then we lived through the "step by step" experience of watching and hearing of your progress during the transition. The bouts with the psychiatrist, the beginning of hormones, the school complications, new career, changing public restrooms, name change, changing from F to M on your driver license — all necessitated by your transition and recognition of your true gender. The break up of your long relationship with your partner was, I know, very difficult, as well as selling a home you loved. But you did it and handled it all very well.

You now seem to me to be happier and more confident in your outlook. You are holding and advancing in a good job. Buying another house was, perhaps, a scary decision, but one which certainly makes economic sense. Now, three years (is it that long?) after your decision to transition, you seem to have a stable, and I hope, happy life. How wonderful!

The point of this letter is that I want to say, "Thank you, Allen. Thank you for insisting on being who you are, and opening our eyes to greater truths than we knew before." I do not believe I can truly realize how great an effort this must have been for you. I respect you for making yourself go up this difficult road. I am impressed that you knew this was the right thing for you to do, and did it. I admire you for facing each difficulty in your chosen (no, not chosen, necessary) path and, with your now well-exercised equanimity, overcoming it and moving on again. Your struggle with your life and the quest to be who you are has been an object lesson in how to live, and how to deal with life, using to the best advantage the cards you are dealt. I am proud you are my son. I just want you to really understand that.

> I love you,
> Dad

MOM, DAD, WE NEED TO TALK
Anne Samson*

I'm a child of the '60s, have MA's in Humanities and History, and am a technical writer. I've been married thirty years (amazing!), with two kids, two dogs, one cat. My hobbies are reading (regional novels, philosophy and religions, cookbooks), cross stitch and quilting, walking, playing with friends (including my husband), gardening, discovering new music. My philosophy is Live and Let Live.

Ever since I can remember I've felt something was wrong, but it wasn't until about a year ago that I figured out what it was. Our first-born son, Paul, home from his freshman year in college, began for us the painful and rewarding journey of being trans-parents and this is how we reacted.

Our responses to our child were probably predictable, and probably less than praiseworthy. Are you sure (this is not just your over-active imagination)? Is it possible that you're gay (and just don't want to face it or think we'll accept it)? Is it because you haven't had any sexual experience or close male/female relationships (and are somewhat fearful of getting into them)? And so on. We came up with every alternative explanation we could think of in order not to have to deal with the unthinkable proposition that our intelligent, sensitive, highly talented firstborn son would have to spend the rest of his/her life coping with a condition only those who have it know much about. I certainly didn't. My image of transgendered people came from TV and movie images of transvestites; at the time, I didn't know the difference.

But you liked trucks, we pleaded. You used to play at being Spiderman and Batman. You were always making Star Wars light sabers and Star Trek laser guns. How can this be? Of course it was also true that as a baby, this child sat on the floor and chatted to the pots and pans, begged me for a swimsuit like my pretty flowered one, and argued emphatically with her dad that she was a girl and not a boy. (We decided that at age two she just didn't have it all straight yet, and dropped the subject, assuming eventually she'd figure it out).

So many almost unnoticed incidents that we dismissed because they didn't make sense at the time began to fall into place: Paul asking me to teach her to sew, the detailed costumes she made for role-playing games and the unisex or female characters she always played; the interest in relationships, both her own and other peoples; the fact that she had friends of both sexes but never dated, the hatred of sharing a room at camp or in the college dorm. I understood now the depression she went through in junior high and why she went to such lengths to wear the most shapeless and drab clothes. As she explained, she always thought she might grow up to be a woman, but in junior high she had to face the fact that wasn't going to happen. The rush of memories was overwhelming. I was torn between It can't be so and Here's another indication that it is.

No one tells you that when a child turns out to be totally other than you assumed, it is very much like a death. Not that parents of trans people are the only ones who experience this grief, but it is peculiar in that there is often no one around who understands the details and can share similar experiences. What I would have given to know just one trans parent in that first year! In our small town, there is still an element of disgrace in being sexually different than the mainstream; people who will talk about their children doing drugs will not mention that their child is gay, if they even know. To whom can you say, Well, I used the pronoun "she" for the first time today?

So many feelings accompany a parent's initial adjustment. There is the fear, What will this mean for my child and her future? There is anger and sadness that you didn't know and didn't guess. There is grief at the loss of dreams; the future becomes a blank because none of the ordinary expectations for a son or daughter necessarily apply. For me there is still sadness that we didn't get to share many of the ordinary mother-daughter things that are so much a part of a daughter's growing up. The inevitable question, Is it something I did? haunted us. Transgenderedness challenges the black and white assumptions we all make about our sexuality, a basic fact of our identity. Was I wrong in teaching her how to sew? Could there be a gender-disorder strain in our family tree? There was almost no literature in the local library to answer these questions, and we knew nothing about the Internet, even if we had had access to it.

Fortunately, a few trusted friends and our son-now-daughter, Marie, came to the rescue. Marie provided us with articles she'd received from a trans support group in a nearby large city. She even took me to a meeting where I got to meet, not the flashy transvestites I'd seen on TV, but real, live children, husbands, and wives who talked honestly about the challenges and joys of their daily lives, and who spoke compassionately about us, their friends and family. The information I gained from them helped immeasurably both in my own adaptation and in explaining to friends and family who were as ignorant as I was. The most important fact, and the one least understood, is that being a trans is not a choice; it is a self-discovery.

Adapting to our child's new identity was a challenge for our couple relationship. For a long time we were unable to talk about it with each other in much detail. My reaction was to want to talk endlessly about the revelation, search for information, and speculate on the causes and consequences. My husband's way of dealing with difficult material has always been not to talk much about it until he settles it in his own mind. At some point we each trusted long time friends with the information, and from there the circle gradually extended, as Marie's initial revelation rippled through family and friends.

The hardest task was telling family, immediate and extended. Endless questions bubbled up. How will this affect our other child?

What will the extended family's reaction be? Will they reject me or my child because of this revelation? We asked Marie to tell the family she felt she wanted to tell, as we figured that was both her prerogative and also good practice for a string of future explanations. Our son, younger by two years, took the news without much outward reaction. As a late teenager, he had his own life to live and was pretty immersed in it. Like his father, he processes things slowly, but he nearly always comes out on the side of love and inclusion.

Marie's grandmother was concerned, but accepting. My husband's brother was puzzled. My two sisters were incensed, blaming companions, rebellion, or denial about homosexuality. That Marie was the first child in the extended family, and that they had doted on him/her for years made the revelation hard for them to accept. Also, they didn't see Marie often enough to get used to this new person emerging from her cocoon. To their credit, they have come to accept the fact that Paul is now Marie. They are not comfortable conversing about the subject, but they are all polite and do care about her, despite the fact they think she must be nuts to live as female and to plan to undertake surgery.

In the beginning, my own communication with Marie about the subject was not much more extensive than that of my sisters. Rather than inundate her with the confused storm of feeling I experienced at first, I chose instead to confide in a trusted friend and in my husband. This allowed me to express the fear and anger more freely. I didn't want to say things to Marie I might later regret, and I wanted to move through my selfish concerns to some position from which I could relate to Marie hereafter. What it finally came down to was that, in a choice between my cherished ideas of my child and a relationship with the child herself, I would much rather have the latter. One doesn't quit loving just because the lovee turns out not to be the person you thought he was.

Eventually Marie and I did have the relief of talking together about that initial time. It was a difficult period for both of us, I think. I hadn't realized, nor maybe had she, that we would have to develop a whole new relationship. Nor had I realized that she would have to go through all the stages from early teen to her current age, as she worked to get through the female socialization she missed as a male teenager. Again I was faced with myself. I did not enjoy being a 13-year-old female, myself, and I did not enjoy learning to relate to one. Luckily, we both made it through that phase.

I can now report that it is possible for both children and parents to survive that difficult first few years of trans adjustment. As parents, we may have lost a son, but we have gained a daughter who seems much happier and more spontaneous than she did before. I like to think that we as parents have gained in tolerance and compassion as we struggled to rethink our assumptions about gender identity and sexuality. Despite our fears for her future and her difficult time searching for a job in our city, Marie has begun a career on the west coast, and is enjoying the freedom she finds there. We talk weekly, exchanging information about books, cooking, decorating, and upcoming events. Probably I'm less tempted than I might have been to offer advice. Having never parented a trans child before, I am not aware of any norms that one should abide by. We pretty much concentrate on the present as it unfolds.

At some point, Marie plans to go for surgery and although I have some fears, I feel that Marie and we will deal with whatever transpires. I have seen her exhibit great courage and determination as she works to make a life for herself. I am very proud to have such an amazing child.

HEALING THROUGH ART
Linda Milligan

I am a Registered, Board-Certified Art Therapist. I have lectured and written about art therapy and currently work with 14 - 18 year old males in a maximum security institution. My husband, Pat, our two cats, and I make our home in New Jersey.

Art expression is an important part of my life's journey and I rely on it to help me express and work through life's unexpectd turns. My art during my child's gender change from female to male was usually done rapidly in tempera paint. The paint was thick, with lots of movement and many deep colors. I found myself enjoying the feel of the paint, exploring its qualities as I explored new and old ideas about my relationship with my child. The images are of people, sometime naked, and at other times color and designs were added to express conflict, confusion and pain. The thick lines round the people are there to hold in and separate feelings...

My feelings as expressed in my art were similar to the feelings experienced during the grief process: shock, denial, isolation, anger, depression and acceptance. I share my art with the hope that the reader may gain a deeper connection to the images than they could to the words.

HELP!

With paintings, as with dreams, the maker is often all the parts within the image. I am the stunned female, the small child needing comfort and protection, and the cold, angry, rejecting adult. These feelings are also the feelings I feel from my child. The colors in the painting are strong. The lines are thick, holding each figure together, keeping the feelings safely contained.

MOTHER AND CHILD

I love my child; we are connected. Did I miss some behavior that explains this change? I spend time looking at old pictures, remembering, holding onto the past.

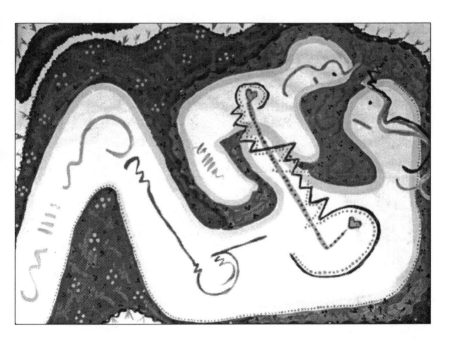

FEATS OF DARING

This painting is one of my favorites, a symbolic expression of letting go and acceptance. The public performance of a daring act is a metaphor for the courage my child needed to begin the very visual process of change. The circus theme permits me to separate my feelings, playfully, and begin to let go of my daughter. That, too, feels like a daring act.

WE ARE A FAMILY

The small precious child I remember holding in my arms, laughing, crying and playing with, is still there. This is my child and I love him. The colors are lighter and brighter now. The lines around the forms, thinner, and the background is calmer. I am calmer and brighter, as I begin to realize my fears are unfounded. I see my child growing happier and I am more comfortable with seeing a son.[4]

OUR GENDER FAMILY
Rachel Miller

I am a heterosexual, married man with a professional position, a respected member of the community. No one would ever guess that I'm a transvestite. For many years I suppressed my true self, but, in desperation, began a quest for relief as described in "The Bliss of Becoming One!" (Rainbow Books, 1996). I am a regular writer, activist, speaker and publisher of Our Gender Family a quarterly Email newsletter.

Hey, Mom! Would you like another manhattan?

Once I understood and accepted my propensity to cross-dress, I was determined to end the hypocrisy of hiding that part of myself from my loved ones. I had come out to my wife, sister and a few others with great success in early 1994. I wanted to tell my mother, but she lived in a small Wisconsin town 1,700 miles away. It was crucial to do it in person and my chance came with a business conference in Chicago in June. I made arrangements to drive up to my Mom's house on Friday afternoon.

My Mom and I have had an excellent relationship for many years. Still, I was fearful of her response. I knew that I couldn't continue to live a lie any longer, yet I had heard enough stories to know that there was significant risk in telling. Much of the advice I had received from well-intentioned transvestites was to NEVER TELL ANYONE! Perhaps my greatest concern was her religious background. My Mom is an extraordinarily devout Catholic and attends Mass daily. I had never heard a sermon that preached tolerance towards cross-dressers, so my anxiety level was high.

One thing I had learned in telling others is to take control of the situation rather than letting things happen by chance. So, after a great dinner of fresh lake perch I took advantage of a Wisconsin characteristic and my Mom's one small vice — brandy. Most people think of Wisconsin as the beer-swilling capital but it's in the consumption of brandy where we are true professionals. In the evening Mom enjoys a brandy manhattan (2 parts brandy + 1 part sweet vermouth, for the uninitiated) on the rocks.

My butterflies disappeared with the first drink and the beginnings of courage arrived with the second. Before the third, I thought I'd better start telling my story or risk losing the ability to speak rationally. "So Mom, I've got something I'd really like to tell you." I had developed a pattern of presenting a personalized letter to each person we were going to tell. It was designed to establish the desired context for the discussion. Here's a lightly edited version of the one I gave my Mom:

"Dear Mom,

"Over the years you have sent birthday and holiday cards that express the most wonderfully thoughtful sentiments. It makes me feel very good to know that you feel that way about me. I have always felt that we were very much alike with our softness and sensitivity. I like that part of me. Unfortunately, I was also insecure and uncertain and others often took advantage of me. So, far from being settled, life has been a long journey of exploring and finding out who I am and who I want to be.

"The big improvements started on Easter Sunday, 1980 when I first attended a new Church and with the help of many, began to discover my spiritual and emotional self. It was the beginning of a long journey to become all I am capable of being.

"Over the years I made great progress. Still, I continued to have difficulty with one area of my life. That one area is often viewed negatively by others so it was difficult for me to deal with it. Finally, on my 50th birthday, I determined that no matter how difficult the process might be, I was going to resolve it.

"My search turned out far better than I had ever envisioned. As a result I feel whole and complete for the first time in my life. My big questioning and searching is over. The best part is that I like the person I found inside myself.

"The attached poem is a way to tell my story simply. What the poem says may surprise you, and it may take awhile to get used to, but it is all positive. I am glad, finally, to be able to share my feelings with you. We can talk about any parts that you are comfortable discussing.

"Mostly, I just want to say - I love you!

"Your son, Richard"

The poem that I shared with her is an outgrowth of trying to put my cross-dressing in perspective. Without the appropriate context it could appear to be the defining characteristic of my life. While I am a cross-dresser, that is just one aspect. There are, also, many other important aspects to my personality. I wrote the poem for myself but found it effective in communicating the whole me to others. Here's a copy of what I gave her.

Do you love me?

You know me as a person who has strong spiritual beliefs,
who loves his wife and is committed to his marriage,
who values family and friends, and
who feels that being a grandfather is one of the greatest
    experiences of life.

You know me as a person who loves children and childlike things,
who is sensitive, caring and compassionate,
who believes in personal responsibility, and
who is committed to working hard and doing a good job.

You know me as a person who enjoys good food and fine wines
(plus beer, pizza and ice cream),
who brings humor to the workplace and elsewhere,
who works at physical conditioning and enjoys long distance running,
and who loves animals, especially cats.

You know me as a person who is discovering a love for theater
and the arts,
who is learning to express his enjoyment of decorating, colors,
fabrics and textures,
who wants to be accepted and loved just as he is,
so, do you love me?

What if I take a chance and become vulnerable and disclose my
story;
will you still love me?

What if society does not accept part of me, but I do;
will you still love me?

What if I need to expose the truth about me to be at peace inside;
will you still love me?

What if I told you that I like to shave my legs and wear a skirt;
will you still love me?

As I handed the poem to her, she started reading and I stopped
breathing. At the end she put the paper down and said, "Of course I
love you. I don't understand all this, but I love you." She asked a
few questions and we talked for about a half hour. Finally she stopped
and asked me to follow her into her bedroom. She opened her jewelry box and asked if there was anything I wanted for myself. I was

thrilled with her response. I took a necklace plus a locket with my grandparents' pictures inside. Then she opened her closet and asked if I wanted any clothes. I laughed and said, "Mom, we're not anywhere close to the same size but THANK YOU!" We hugged and all was right in my world. No more manhattans were required.

Well, that's my story. What's the best way to start coming out of your closet?[5]

PART III

INVENTIVE LOVE RELATIONSHIPS

CATERPILLAR TO BUTTERFLY
Jackie Greer

I met Michael while in high school and we married shortly after I graduated with a degree in journalism. I worked as a reporter, section editor, and am now a personal banker with a major credit-card company, seeking to return to full-time writing and editing. I enjoy reading, walking, and cooking. Michael works for the State of California and transitioned to Stephanie while in the same position. Our daughter, Shelly, was adopted as a newborn.

I see a beautiful butterfly emerging. The caterpillar was nice and I miss him, but the butterfly is so gentle, so peaceful, so softly radiant, that I almost don't remember the warm, fuzzy, little guy. The butterfly will be so wonderful once her wings are fully spread into the sun.

Being the spouse of a male-to-female transsexual has forced me to embark on a journey parallel to hers—examining who I am, what I need, and, most of all, confronting my definition of love and what I meant when I took my wedding vows twenty years ago.

Who am I? I can no longer define that in terms of being a wife. I went from submissive daughter, trying to be daddy's and mommy's girl as well as a replacement for the son they lost in 1963, to an equally submissive wife, happily letting Michael make the decisions and deferring to his leadership. I still believe that the husband should take authority over his household, his wife and children, and set the spiritual tone of the home. The wife, I believe, is the quiet strength and keel that keeps the household running, regaining strength from her husband as needed.

When Michael told me almost three years ago that he needed to explore his femininity, I suddenly realized what had attracted me to him in the first place. It was Stephanie shining through. I saw her reflected in Michael's gentleness, kindness, caring, and sensitivity. I always knew he was special; I saw then that the specialness was Stephanie. After that conversation over lunch at Fresh Choice I felt shaken but peaceful, and Michael seemed giddy with joy.

The next two years are a blur; they were a vortex sweeping us and our daughter Shelly through a maze of emotions, discoveries and changes that happened faster than I ever dreamed. Michael broke down at work, then spent most of one summer upstairs in our room curled up on our bed alternately staring and crying. Shelly escaped to summer school and the pool. I escaped primarily to my job at a women's clothing store.

I was so proud as I watched Michael gain enough strength to return to work, and sat next to him as he revealed his transsexuality to his co-workers. My brother visited in November and I matter-of-factly told him. He was supportive, but, I think, angry on Shelly's behalf. My most frightening moment, then my greatest relief, came when I told my parents a month later. They acknowledged they were scared for Shelly and me, but understood how necessary the change was. I felt like the weight of the world was off my shoulders and I was so proud of the two strongest people I know.

Stephanie has been living full time for almost a year now. These last months have been painful, as I have allowed myself to grieve the loss of normalcy, the loss of the Donna Reed family life that was the envy of our neighbors. I have had to bear much of Shelly's anger over the loss of her dad. The greatest pain for me is knowing I can't supply her a dad; nor can I supply Stephanie what she seems to need most—a strong pair of male arms.

But I have gained so much; I feel a joy and peace deeper than I have ever known. I have been tested and proven. I have taken love beyond pretty words spoken in a white dress, taken it to the level of helping someone with a penis pick out dresses and select the right makeup colors—and I've had a ball doing it! Stephie is the sister I never had and always wanted. The choice became simple: I want the person who loves and cares for me, although no longer in a traditional relationship. I have gained a great freedom. I no longer feel pressure to meet someone else's need for femininity as I did with Michael; Stephanie can now enjoy her own femininity openly, and I am proud to help her.

I have discovered strength, endurance and commitment I never thought I possessed. I am finding the courage to build my own world, where I am dependent only upon God and the strength He has given me. That discovery is infinitely rewarding. I need Stephie. My daughter needs her. We three need one another.

I pray other spouses and partners can see the opportunity for growth that living with a transgendered person presents. My commitment is stronger than ever. The pain is worthwhile. It can lead you to your own new world.

Love and Prayers,
JG

~~~~~~~~~~

No pessimist ever discovered the secrets of the stars or sailed to an uncharted land or opened a new heaven to the human spirit.
— Helen Keller   (Raquel Rice)

THE WOMAN WITHOUT A PAST
Janis Wagemans

I studied at the Amsterdam Artacademy and currently work with mentally handicapped people. My partner, Renate (Natasja), and I published a column together during Renate's transition and have recently registered as life partners under The Netherland's new law. Renate has also written a novel and several short stories.

I take another sip of my drink and watch my love sleeping around the corner. She breathes out calmly, with little puffs. Is she dreaming? When I first met her she dreamt a lot about violence, police, and dead friends. She often awoke screaming. Now I can't even remember the last time this happened; she has been sleeping well for a long time now. So well she no longer needs sleeping pills.

It has become almost dark. Thank God we don't have to get up early beause tomorrow is Wednesday, my day off. With my glass in one hand I turn out the little lamp in the corner. I take a seat on the bench across from Natasja and watch her face. Her skin looks pretty good; tomorrow the electrolycist will remove the last bristly hairs. Natasja will be relieved at not having to shave any more. A historical moment! We have had many such moments lately.

We were so happy when the Civil Registrar's letter came saying Natasja is now a woman — legally! How proud we were when she got her new passport! Looking at the picture she couldn't help smiling, telling me that she looked like the average "worn-out housewife."

There will be two more years of electrolycis on Natasja's face, the dark hairs may be gone but there will be more, thinner and lighter hairs, growing back in different layers. Natasja pulls them out daily with a pair of tweezers and a magnifying mirror.

I saw a photocolage recently in my brother's living room. Behind me, on the bench, sits my friend, a man in his forties with a few gray hairs and a pair of round glasses on his nose. He has put a hand on my shoulder; between the fingers of the other he holds a burning cigarette. Despite the friendly laugh at the photographer his eyes show sadness. His features tell that he used to be a handsome man, but clearly he is fading in this photo.

Having a joint past is dear to me. Memories of meeting and parting, of love letters, beautiful moments or even bad ones make the bond all the stronger. But sometimes it seems like the past is playing tricks on us. I don't have pictures of Natasja when we first met, and I know I will never find them. When I look at the ones I have I see a familiar face, the face of somebody I used to love. Natasja's face is not on them, beause the sad man she used to be died — slowly. That mousey man is now a ravishing blond beauty, a self-aware liberated woman. That's wonderful, but scary, too.

I remember that important breakthrough evening, two years ago now. We were meditating... I had put out the light in our livingroom, but instead of going to bed directly I lit a stick of incense. I sat behind Natasja on the floor, holding her tight in my arms, and rocked her gently. We dreamt with our eyes open, and in our fantasy I took her to a deserted beach. I started to describe us, and it was very clear that Natasja had a woman's body! I saw her lying in my arms, dressed in a breathtaking short red dress. Her bare legs were tanned, the wet sand was fixed, sparkling on her breastbone. Her breasts were firm and wet, shiny, provocative in the half opened dress. We became excited, but that wasn't all... Natasja suddenly started to cry. I can still picture us sitting there in the dark, and I know how powerless I felt.

Not long after that, Natasja finally made the big decision: she now knew that she wasn't a transvestite or "just a feminine man" as she had thought all these years. Had to think, in order to keep every-one that she loved satisfied, and to maintain her home and some suc-cess in her work. After all these years the truth was undeniably strong; she was a woman! She had always been one, but she had done every-thing to forget. She didn't need to ask others 'what am I?' any more, she figured it out by herself.

I know how we sat together in the hospital restaurant two weeks later, eating a large piece of chocolate cake to celebrate the green light to take hormones and to start the Real Life Trial. This little event became a tradition every three months, when we had to return for physical check-ups and to see the psychologist. We celebrated every phase, no matter how difficult it had been. But, my God, it was hard to accept that Natasja's libido decreased rapidly (due to taking hormones), and that we got into an almost platonic relationship. We, who used to be such passionate lovers!

And it became even harder when I realized half way through the Real Life Trial that I really was a lesbian, instead of the bisexual girl I imagined I was. Imagined, because I never slept with a girl before Natasja. Even though I had called our love "lesbian" from the begin-ning, it was from the perspective of a gorgeous but closeted trans-vestite and hir "maidenprince." I discovered my true sexuality while she was captured within a sealed body. It created a lot of tension, especially when I felt temporarily attracted to another woman. I never cheated, but I felt guilty nevertheless.

I put my glass back on the table. Natasja is still fast asleep. I am glad that we always remained honest with each other. How frustrat-ing and painful the process could be for the two of us, but speaking about our insecurities and fears brought many good things in the end.

She is twenty years older than I, something I always found attrac-tive. But, like everything else, this aspect, too, has another side, because Natasja had lived half a life before we met. She was married at the time, trying hard to be a man, raising two daughters with her former wife. Ruby, their youngest, is twelve. She likes me a lot, and her stay with us is usually warm and cozy. Needless to say, however, being a child of parents who divorced quite suddenly really shook her world. It was maybe even harder for her than the announcement of Natasja's fulltime existence. At one time during the RLT, Ruby said to Natasja, "I was used to your wearing women's clothes ever since I can remember. Now you are really becoming a woman. We both are!"

Natasja's greatest loss is undoubtedly her relationship with Tanya, the teenage daughter whom she raised from the age of four. Tanya's biological father rarely looked after his child until she was old enough to look after herself. But today the cards are shuffled differently. Tanya saw the grief of her mother caused by the divorce, and got furious at Natasja. She has never spoken, or written, to us ever again. The man who never wiped her nose, nor sent birthday cards, for that matter, was now her hero.

It took Ruby only a few months to change 'his' to 'her' and to say 'Natasja' instead of 'daddy'. Natasja asked her to try changing this after an incident at the bakery. The man behind the counter asked if we needed anything else, and Ruby asked, turning her head towards Natasja (beautifully dressed in jeans and a white blouse, make up on her face) "Dad, can I have a croissant?". The man looked at us with a slightly bewildered gaze, but nothing else happened.

It must have been hard for Ruby to lose a father, but she seldom opens up about it. Whenever we try to raise the subject she gets a headache and goes to bed. She is the kind of girl who wants to see everyone happy, without having to deal with difficult issues. It's not just her age, it's part of her personality, too. We try not to push her to open up; she can take all the time that she needs.

At the very beginning of her transition Natasja got lots of strange looks, and had many misunderstandings. ("Can I help you sir? Ehm... madam?") But that's all in the past now; nobody makes that mistake anymore. Strangers haven't got a clue that she was born a male. As a boy at the age of four she used to dress herself with her sister's clothes. Back then, in the late fifties there was no room for such "filthy" things. (She learned pretty early that it was bad to wear girl's clothes.)

Natasja sighs deeply and turns over on the bed. I can see the old scars in the hollow of her arm, permanent reminders of her previous life in the gutter. She kicked a severe drug addiction at the age that I am now. Seven years she lived on the streets of Amsterdam, more dead then alive. Stealing and lying, to feed this great hunger. It might be too tempting to reduce it all to her inner conflict, but still I really believe she tried to silence the screaming voice inside of her...She has done almost everything to be that real man, and sometimes it worked a while. Women fell easily in love with this stout James Dean lookalike, but all the one night stands in the world couldn't make the confusion go away. Natasja has been clean for twenty years now, and our relationship is exclusive. Her anxiety disappeared forever on that memorable day in December last year.

* * *

I'm sitting on a chair next to Natasja's empty bed. The sun is shining in the room. Everything is quiet on the hallway, and at the nursing station. When I ask at half past one if the surgery is done yet, a nurse tells me that 'Miss Stoute has been in the recovery room since one o'clock.'

She must be cold when she wakes up. Would she have awakened already? The nurse who accompanies us this morning enters the room. She pulls a bed aside. She turns towards me and says: "Well, we'll go get Natasja, you can come along if you like." Of course I want to! I walk behind her and feel like I'm in fog. The white dress of the nurse goes before me as a beacon of light. Hallways, doors, green shiny floors. The nurse enters the recovery room and points to a corner I can't see. She asks for "Miss Stoute". I stay at the hallway, don't dare to move. The door closes automatically. I wait.

When it opens again I see two nurses. They push the bed with Natasja on it. She sees me. With some difficulty she raises her head a little and says: "Hi Djezz, here I am!"

I get up and walk towards my sleeping beauty. I give her a soft kiss on her forehead and wake her gently. It is time to go to bed.

Letter to my Wife

Darling, I kissed the real you for the very first time today. It made us both cry. You waited so long to become whole, and so did I.

Now we may, can, finally exist as the women we really are. Our future will be magnificent!

Not because nothing bad will ever happen to us again, or as you often say, "Don't expect that it will rain flowers from the sky," because life remains the same. The future will be great because a flame has been lit within us.

The last couple of months, maybe even years, we were not always able to achieve the most from ourselves, though I do believe we both lived and worked as well as we knew how.

Now we have the chance to grow, to embrace the world, and to be there for others. Our energy has no limits any more. No real boundaries. We can breathe deeply, fill our lungs with air! We will live as we always imagined in our dreams — really live!

My darling, I am truly happy. Together we will grow old, hand in hand. I'm looking forward to creating such a past.

With love,
Your Girlprince

A SPOUSE'S STAGES OF GRIEF
Sandy Deyo

My husband is a preoperative transsexual. We have been married for 28 years and are still good friends. I wrote this article when I first realized what was happening— and still used male pronouns and "husband" to describe my spouse. My writing helped me find a sense of direction on how to let go and it has helped others. We have come a long way, together, since I wrote this.

Going through the transgender process with one's spouse is often like going through the five stages of grief: denial, anger, bargaining, depression and acceptance. Some of the feelings may be mixed together and overlapping, but they are all there. For me it was like being with someone who had a terminal illness. I think the goal for all relationships should be wanting each other to be happy and healthy. The transgender process can put tremendous stress on both of you. Each is trying to help make it easier on the other.

Through the years I never thought anything like this could happen. We had a good marriage with true love and commitment. With all the problems our friends had and the high divorce rate, I felt I was lucky to have a spouse like him.

Then I begin to suspect there was a transgender problem. Thinking back, there were signs and signals all along, but I DENIED they existed. His putting on my make-up was fun, something to do that did not cost any money, and it was only the two of us, no harm in that. As the marriage progressed, so did the process. There were several months between episodes, and dressing in my clothes was fun at first, but then I became concerned. Later he was dressing whenever opportunity presented itself, usually when I was gone. But I knew.

Later, the opportunities became more frequent and he would ask "Do you mind?" I would say okay and then leave (out of sight, out of mind), still denying that any problem existed. Just as in the case of the illness, as things progress one can no longer deny that something is happening. So I said to myself, "Face it." Right, but its not that easy.

The news finally came, "Honey, I think I have a gender identity problem." I become ANGRY, felt rejected, like I had been cheated on all these years. "Who have you been making love to all these years?" (Maybe that's a stupid question in the first place. You know the answer is going to be YOU.) It was tough to take. For a period of time I didn't want to be around him. And forget sex! I got scared. If he feels female where do I fit in? I began to question my own sexuality. I believed I might be the cause. Maybe if I were more female or a better wife this would not have happened. As in a terminal illness one questions — why me? What did I do to deserve this?

I started BARGAINING with God to change things. I will dress sexier, I will initiate sex more. I will be a better wife — just tell me what you want me to do. Just as one might with any pending loss, I wanted things back the way they were. All this did not work, so what's next?

DEPRESSION. Besides all the other stress in my life THIS HAS TO HAPPEN. I was already stressed over other problems that I blamed on myself. Depression got to me. I could not talk without crying. I went to work, but did only what had to be done. I locked myself up, thinking I was the only person going through this. I had to get help; I could not go through this by myself. The difference with this problem and terminal illness is that with an illness one has family, friends, coworkers for support and there is cooperation, always someone to talk to. Later I found there IS help out there for my kind of problem. It may not be as readily available at first, but it's there.

I finally came to grips with this terrible "problem.". I ACCEPTED that it was not my fault and it was happening anyway. (Always in the back of my mind was a thought or hope for a cure, so to speak, and new ideas kept popping into my head. Sometimes I even acted on them .) Maybe I should try again to be more sexy. It didn't help the over-all problem, but I could forget it for a while and relieve some stress. What really helped? Honesty, expressing my feelings openly. ASKING QUESTIONS. Why? How? When? I sought information that would help explain what was happening. This was a long process, sometimes interrupted.

I always held to the goal that, as in any relationship, real love means wanting one's partner to be happy and healthy. Then, with both of us committed to each other, we would work hard to obtain that goal.

~~~~~~~~~~

Allen once played violin in a lesbian string quartet. When he began his FTM transition he felt it necessary to explain himself to the lead player. After hemming and hawing and finally saying he was a transsexual, the lead said, without blinking, "Oh, is that all. I thought you were going to tell me you were switching to bassoon or something!" (Mary Boenke)

BIRTHING NEW LIFE
Loree Cook-Daniels

I own WordBridges, a consulting firm specializing in conflict resolution and written communications. Marcelle, my partner of fifteen years, is a female-to-male transsexual, who transitioned after bearing our child. We live with our son, Kai, in Vallejo, California.

It's one of the few regrets I have, that pregnancy.

It was a much-wanted pregnancy. It took fifteen months of trying, after more than a year and a half of negotiating, after seven years of fantasizing and mentally trying things on for size. And, of course, we'd never regret having the result of the pregnancy, our wonderful child, Kai.

But the pregnancy itself was awful. Just thinking about it makes me tear up, four years after the fact.

* * * *

At first, I thought Marcelle was joking. After all, on the morning he woke me to say he'd decided to have our baby, the calendar said April 1st. But he wasn't fooling and, in fact, it was our best option. We believed my hormonal cycle too erratic to make insemination very feasible, and I had no desire to bear a child anyway. The adoption option seemed foreclosed. Every Gay and Lesbian family we spoke to who had successfully adopted told us that the <u>only</u> way it could be done was for everyone to pretend the relationship was just roommates. We didn't see how that would work for us, an interracial Lesbian couple who had taken the in-your-face step of legally ensuring we had the same last name. Even the most denial-facile social worker and judge wouldn't be able to see their way around that particular signal that we were slightly more than roommates.

And, to be truthful, we thought the pregnancy might do Marcelle good. We had wanted a child so long that having Marcelle's hated female body produce such a miracle might, we thought, help him appreciate it more.

We were wrong. Terribly wrong.

For nine months, Marcelle had trouble keeping a meal down. He actually lost weight, although the baby found enough nourishment from existing stocks to come out, full-term, at nearly 6 pounds. But it wasn't just the nausea, or even the scary bleeding, that was the problem. It was that being pregnant, for Marcelle, was profoundly wrong. He was not meant to endure those emotions, those inabilities, those...oh lord, most of all those...awful comments from others about how expectant mothers should act.

Suddenly thrust into the unfamiliar role of butch, I did my best to be supportive of this cranky, sick, depressed pregnant "wife." But I was also struggling and angry. After nine years of blocking Marcelle's transition, telling him he must choose either surgery or me, I had finally come to my senses. The turning point had been two lines in a film we saw at the local Lesbian and Gay film festival. A female-to-male transsexual said that he had had trouble coping with his transsexual feelings because he really didn't like men. Then one day, he said, he realized that not all genetic men like men as a class, either.

It was my turning point, too. Marcelle's misanthropy had always been one of my primary sticking points. I couldn't imagine it was healthy to want to become something you clearly didn't like. But our friend, Max, was right: men, as a class, in our society are not necessarily worth emulating. But that doesn't mean one can't intend to, and be, a better sort of man.

Walking home from the film, I asked Marcelle if he still thought about transitioning. His answer, given the years in which the topic had occupied our house unbroached, was stunning.

"Every day."

I took a few more silent, faltering steps, reeling with the implications of those two words. How much pain I must have caused my lover and partner for all those years.

"Then I need to step out of your way," I finally, quietly, said.

Given that this conversation came after we had found a donor, negotiated all our legal agreements, and begun inseminating, my sudden change of heart meant revisiting some previous decisions. Marcelle decided he wanted to continue trying to get pregnant, and our donor said he had so little invested in gender that it didn't bother him any that one of the mothers of his child might well morph into another father to his child. So those potential barriers melted away.

But unexpectedly having that immovable obstacle called Loree cleared from his path turned out to confuse Marcelle. After two decades and more of dreaming of being male, he suddenly discovered that my opposition had completely overshadowed and hidden his own doubts, which now came out to bedevil us both. He couldn't, simply stated, decide for sure whether or not to transition.

Which made me nuts. Especially when we finally had a confirmed pregnancy, I needed to know: was my partner going to be male or female? Was my child going to have two mothers, or a mother and a father? Marcelle had to decide now, I frequently fumed aloud, because I didn't want my child to be confused by a parent's sex change. Marcelle would have to transition, I demanded, if he transitioned at all, shortly after the child's birth.

And so the pregnancy went. Marcelle coped badly, physically and emotionally. I veered crazily between trying to be supportive, feeling guilty over Marcelle's difficult pregnancy and my long opposition to his dream, and being angry that he could now not decide if he wanted to live that dream.

By the time Marcelle went into labor, we were already worn out. And we were completely unprepared for what finally emerged from his womb —a boy, after months of completely trusting the doctor's sonogram interpretation that we were expecting a girl!

"What did you say it was?" Marcelle reportedly asked the nurses each time he emerged from the anesthesia. "Did I dream you said it was a boy?" Yes, they assured him, it's a healthy boy. He kept nodding off again, reeling from the implications.

By the time we three left the hospital days later, Marcelle had come to see Kai's unexpected gender as the universe's unmistakable signal. Kai was supposed to be a girl but turned out to be a boy, just like his Dad.

* * * *

Every birth creates at least three new lives. The child's life starts, of course, but his parents' lives alter, too, often so dramatically as to warrant a new designation.

In my case, Kai's birth made me not only a mother, but a wife. It made Marcelle not only a parent, but a man. Kai's birth changed our family from being a couple of out, activist Lesbian- feminists to a nuclear suburban family of Mommy, Daddy, and baby. Our beliefs and commitments are the same, but what we look like to others and the complex of expectations that comes with that perception, expectations that we must either fulfill or fight, have shifted dramatically. Treading our way through this unexpected and yet not unfamiliar (we grew up in it, after all) ocean of stereotypes about who Marcelle and I are as individuals and as a couple, particularly as we've been adapting to our roles as parents and learning who our new "roommate" is, has been challenging, to say the least. But it has also been invigorating and eye-opening, and we have learned and grown tremendously as a result. All of us are better people, we think, for having navigated these strange waters.

So, although I regret the pregnancy itself, I do not regret the lives it birthed. They were not the lives I expected, but then when do lives — our own or others' — turn out as expected? They are still good lives, filled with love and promise, wonder and mystery.

* * * *

(Four years post pregnancy.) I'm pleased to tell you we've won one! I was, today, granted my step-parent adoption of Kai, along with some ground-breaking "firsts." The judge had to, in essence, agree that Marcelle was legally male, that he and I are legally married, and that it's in Kai's best interest to have the law recognize his birth mother as his father and me as his mother. Our home-done insemination from a known donor also turned out to present some problems, but these, too, were resolved. Finally, Kai put in his second-best life performance as a contrary. (The first was his birth, which was breach, having turned from head down just before delivery.) I'm told the judge smiled at his antics, probably figuring that if I was trying to adopt <u>this</u> kid, I was welcome to him!

Tonight I'm a very embarassed, exhausted, but happy (and legal) mom!

~~~~~~~~~~

To create one's own world takes courage. Georgia O'Keefe (Jackie Greer)

LETTER TO OUR CHILD
Morgan Tharan

I am a queer femme, very happily married to a third gendered person and together we are raising a child within our loving family of friends. I am an at-home parent and love it! I write, paint, and thrive on creativity and challenging questions. This piece is dedicated to my special grandmother, who died while listening to our child say, "I love you, great-grandma."

Dear One, My Precious Child:

I'm writing this letter to you when you're two years old. I hope that when you read these words as an older child they will help you if some of what you take for granted now is challenged by the world beyond our loving family.

For the first hour of your life we did not call you by your birth gender. We made sure everyone in the room referred to you simply as "the baby." We did not want you to feel all of the assumptions of gender in those first moments. It was a very peaceful way to welcome you. Now when people try to peg your gender we simply refer to you by name or call you, "child." It is not easy to expand the boundaries of gender in our society, but we are trying.

As your parents, we hope to teach you about diversity of expression and tolerance; no, not just tolerance — celebration of differences. Your Papa lives between genders. S/he is living in a body that most people would describe as female but s/he moves through daily life in ways that are usually seen as male.

I didn't want you to call me "Mom" or "Mama" because those words always make me think of the way people act like they own children. I do not believe that biology makes family so I was happy to turn to the language of our people and claim "Ima" ('mother' in Hebrew) as the special name you call me. I have been happy with the result. People hear you call me "Ima" and they are not able to quickly put our relationship in a box.

When you were born, Papa really felt uncomfortable with the title of "Mom." Sometimes when you call out "Papa," people get confused. Some people get curious and they are willing to ask questions. Some people seem to become angry. This is the hardest thing for me to deal with. I am so protective of you and your Papa. Your parents are happy when you call out "Papa." Papa feels the special nature of your relationship and at the same time feels comfortable in his/her gender expression — living inbetween. We think that being honest about the complexity of how we feel and who we are will help you learn to ask questions and wonder.

I hope when other people, children and adults, ask about your parents that you'll tell them that we love to hike, that we're caring, and that Papa plays guitar and sings and Ima loves to paint and dance. I hope they will listen.

I dream of a community in which gender is not about being a boy/girl/man/woman. I see gender as the beautiful colored pieces of a kaleidoscope. I hope that as you grow we'll help you put your own pieces together and that you'll be able to express all the amazing parts of yourself. I love you beyond measure, my sweet child, and I'll always remember watching you twirl in a rainbow dress while playing with a truck.

Love,
Ima

DEE AND ANNI'S STORY
Ann Coven

I am a registered nurse and a holistic health practitioner. I am doing stress reduction by massage therapy, currently in Massachusetts. My MTF partner of four years and I have been involved with many trans groups in this area. We're also working to educate professionals about "genderdisorder."

Since my introduction to cross-dressing in the spring of 1995, I have acquired an eye-opening education. I fell in love with an unusually sensitive, considerate, and loving man. Being a nurturer by nature, it has always been my way to want to help people feel better. Then, too, I was exposed to lots of alternative life-styles in San Francisco and it had become easier for me to be open-minded. So, I took into consideration the feminine feelings of my new lover and was pleased that when "Daphne" dressed, he/she felt very good and natural. So Daphne came out of the closet in our private lives — literally my closet, as we were mostly the same size!

For almost two years, I experienced feelings of anguish, frustration and confusion with the dual life. I saw the shame and the guilt imposed by our society's narrow-minded, ignorant and fearful views. I lived through Dee's binging and purging, and impulsive beauty appointments that infurated me because I did not understand. Many times I was cruelly angry.

In September 1996, the emotions were high and I saw no option but to leave the person I loved, again because I did not understand. I was heart broken that issues could not be resolved.

As the spirit has guided me through my life, once again the light brought to my attention an article on cross-dressing in a small New Age news magazine. It brought to David the sense of relief that he was not insane. It visibly relieved him of a great burden. The article led us to the International Foundation for Gender Education, to a broad new world of counselors and to a whole community of transgendered folks, people who could understand and help.

I experienced many feelings these past three years with David/ Dee. As happy as I was for Dee to be out of the closet and freed, I began my own process of grieving the loss of my beloved male companion, the person who had asked me to marry him.

For Dee, who has now been living full time as a woman since November 1996, it was evident that "Gender Dysphoria" was the issue.

For myself, the issues of my own femininity were challenged. The issue of who is my true self is a continuing challenge. I wondered why this had happened to me. I was a devastated shell of a person; my world had crumbled. The issues are so complex that I can really understand why a wife, husband, partner or significant other would not be able to deal with this situation and could just walk out the door.

Much of the hurt, pain and anguish that were Dee's, were also mine. I can only say now that with counseling for myself, and Dee's patience, consideration and understanding of my feelings, I have grown, learned and come to feel acceptance. Life looks much more positive now than it did a year go. It has become more of a privilege to share in this interesting life experience. It would be good if I could help someone else come to a similar understanding and accptance. It may be a difficult situation, but it has been an education and an opportunity for me to open my mind to a new frontier...maybe the last frontier ...and quite an adventure.

MORE THAN "STANDING BY MY TRANS"
Trish Nemore

I am 53 years old, have three teenagers, two grown children, and two grandchildren. I would like more time to read, write, play tennis, bake, garden, swim, see movies, and have lunch with friends. I am active in my church, and have worked for more than twenty years as an attorney for low-income older people. I thoroughly enjoy the conversation, exploration and play that is part of the transgender experience.

Summer 1993:

"Have you been shopping together yet and does he have good taste?" This was the instantaneous reply of my dear friend, Barbara, to my half-hour of hemming, stuttering, bumbling confession that I was falling in love with a man who wears women's clothing.

"Bless you, Barbara!" was Pat's response when I called him from a pay phone en route from Hartford, Connecticut to Cambridge, Massachusetts, to report on my visit and conversation.

Spring 1998:

Pat and I have been married for three and a half years, and he is "out" to the whole world. I had known Pat as a possible partner for fourteen days when he told me of his transgenderism. I was dumbstruck. I recovered words a few days later sitting on the beach at Nags Head, North Carolina. Quickly arranging with friends to watch my 11-year old son, I raced to the motel room and wrote Pat to say that if I am going to deal with this, I have to see you dressed. That did not actually happen for several months. It was nearly five years ago. The road from there to here has been pretty interesting.

Two critical circumstances got me to a first level of acceptance. First, I was totally love-struck. Pat is the most wonderful human being I have ever known and I was passionately in love with him almost immediately. Since he told me about his cross-dressing right from the start of our relationship, I did not have to deal with the issues of secrecy, discovery and lost trust that invade so many transgender relationships. I could work with the trans information in the context of our budding courtship and blossoming love.

The second factor was my experience with my friend Barbara, through her coming out as a lesbian to her family. I had seen how they chose to love only a part of her — the part they could separate out from her lesbianism. I knew Barbara as a whole person to be wonderful, kind, funny, smart and a great friend. How could I treat Pat as Barbara's family had treated her? If I were going to love him, I wanted to love all of him, not ask him to take a piece of his soul and put it on a shelf in the closet until I was not around.

I needed solid factual experience in learning about and accepting transgender. I read a few books and articles, but mostly I did other things. I decided to shop for Pat. I felt quite awkward at first, look-ing for feminine things for my 6'5" husband. I also felt weird. But I gained some comfort by starting easy. My first purchase was a slightly feminine amethyst ring. Over time, I have moved through other, more strikingly "feminine" jewelry, to lingerie to fancier lingerie to a full skirt and blouse outfit.

There was a quirky period during the early shopping outings when I got a perverse thrill from the "weirdness" of what I was doing — relishing my secret as I perused items of clothing and jewelry. Now, Pat and I shop together openly for feminine clothes and accessories for both of us.

During our first few years together, I rarely saw Pat dressed. Our

95

lives, with jobs, three kids, falling in love, moving in together, adding to our house and getting married, did not leave much private time for secret evenings of dressing. But we had the intimacy of the bedroom and much conversation. I was permitted to experience transgenderism in small bites.

My first meeting with a transgender group — in early 1996 — was exciting, stimulating and surprisingly comfortable. During a rap session including more than twenty people, we heard a little of the story of each person present. I was struck by the understanding that an important portion of each life was lived in secret. When we left the meeting, I was full of desire for conversation about the experience I had just had, and realized that I, too, would have to keep this secret, for a while at least. I couldn't imagine living that way for thirty, forty or fifty years, as nearly everyone in the room had.

The past two years have been intense in the transgender arena as Pat has moved fairly steadily to being more out to the world. First, renewing ties to the transgender group that he had stopped attending after we got together in 1993. Then coming out to the core membership of our church, telling our children, preaching a sermon about transgender and, some months later, coming to church "dressed. " Most of this happened in 1997; it is less intense for me now, but each public appearance, each public claiming, takes an emotional toll on Pat.

His "coming out" affected me in a different and rather interesting way. As people came to know of Pat's transgender, some, I think, viewed me as the saintly spouse, standing by her trans (to adapt from Tammy Wynette), being dutiful, supportive and loving in the face of adversity. When they realized that I was having great fun and finding interest and excitement in the trans world, I became slightly suspect. On the other hand, I have several colleagues at work whose only connection to transgender is through Pat and me, but who are enthusiastic and inquisitive in our conversations.

My outward stumbling block is pronouns. Pat likes to be referred to as "she" when dressed as a "she," and I have trouble doing that. Pat does not have two different personas, s/he has one name, no wig, and wears earrings in both ears all the time. Pat's clothing, except when going to work in the very traditional male professional "uniform," is nearly all androgynous or explicitly feminine. Unlike many many transgendered men (M2F) I have heard spoken of by their significant others, Pat's personality and manner do not transform when s/he puts on a dress. I do not relate to Pat differently depending on what s/he is wearing. In fact, I was aware very early in our relationship that much of what I love in Pat comes from work s/he has done to claim so-called feminine traits. These traits operate regardless of what Pat is wearing. (Pat uses the term "bi-gender," rather than "transgender" to reflect the view that s/he is not "crossing" from one end of a spectrum to the other, but rather is incorporating masculine and feminine into a single person.)

Our joint work involving transgender issues includes recognizing that I have to take things at the pace that is comfortable for me; Pat does not demand that I accept more than I can accept. While, I would like to offer Pat the gift of the situationally-correct pronoun, I need to do so with integrity to my own emotional agenda. I also think there is substance to be teased out of my struggle with the pronouns, in terms of how I process and relate to the transgender experience, but that is the subject for another writing.

I consider myself lucky to be part of this unfolding story of Pat and others claiming their true selves against the norms of a hostile culture. I also consider myself lucky to be doing it in the 1990s, when the environment is not quite as hostile as it used to be, when there are resources that discuss transgender as a phenomenon but not a disease, when there are groups like TGEA, our local transgender group, that provide safe spaces and opportunities to dress, to talk about the transgender experience and to have fun, and when the media is beginning to provide some sympathetic depictions of transgender folk. This is an adventure!

Like any adventure, it is not all fun. There is hard work involved as well. But it is exciting to be sharing the adventure with the TG community and with my loving, thoughtful, beautiful, sexy Pat. (She looks terrific in purple!)

WHAT'S IN A NAME?
Yancey Lowell*

I am a 40 year old Midwest professional and have been married to an MtF transsexual for nineteen years. We have one daughter, age 11. I'm staying with my spouse because I had the good sense to marry my best friend. We have a strong, loving family and love each other dearly.

The fact that my husband, Bob, planned to change his gender and live the rest of his life as Sally was a very difficult thing to adjust to. Those of us who love Bob, or simply respect his right to determine what is best for his own life, struggled to figure out just what this change meant to us and how it would change our lives. We analyzed the relationship and tried to determine if we would have said or done anything differently if we had known that Bob was actually Sally all along. The big sticking point for me in Bob's transition seemed to be the one thing that should have come most easily — the change in name and pronoun. After all, how hard is it to say "Sally" instead of "Bob", or "she" instead of "he"? They're just words, aren't they? Yeah, right.

When my spouse told me that "he" preferred to be called "she", I thought, "Sure, that's easy." Then I learned just how hard it can be. At the beginning of the transition, few other people knew about it, so I could safely stick to "he" for awhile.

As we told more people about it, I found I had to do a quick mental review every time I opened my mouth. "Does this person know? Can they deal with it? Do they know him as 'he' or as 'she'?" (If anyone was having trouble with the whole thing, we overlooked it if we knew they were trying. Everyone needs time to come to terms with something so rare and dramatic.) What became so annoying was the realization that I was doing the mental review before referring to ANYONE at all. I remember laughing out loud when a friend of ours complained that she was doing the review even when speaking of her dad, who certainly had no problems with his masculine identity. That quick, panicked "He? She? Whom am I talking to? What am I talking about?" can drive you crazy. I managed not to despair; it became easier with practice.

The name change can be harder. A person's name becomes a very basic part of that person. Those of us who are parents (or even pet owners, for that matter) can remember saying (or hearing the other parent say), "Well, I like the name, but I knew someone with that name and I didn't like him/her, so let's not use it." A name really can be more than just a word.

When my spouse changed her name, it took a lot of practice to get used to saying it. I felt as though I were trying to fool someone. It was actually easier in public, probably because I DID feel as though I were putting on an act. I can clearly remember the first time I used the name when it was just the two of us. I wasn't aware how much I considered it an "act" until I caught myself thinking "Why am I using that name? There's no one here. Whom are we trying to fool? We both know her real name." This was all a sort of subconscious background noise, but it was there, and it was uncomfortable.

The funny part of all this was that it was so familiar. I have had three friends who have changed their names without changing their genders, and using their new names was just as difficult. Leonard changed his name to Tyrone, Debbie to Joy, and Colleen to Dolly. All of their friends (and presumably their families, too) went through this same "Whom are we trying to fool?" business. You feel silly using the new name, because you all know better. (This is why I never bothered to change my own rather unusual name.) And, of course, many of our married friends change their names, too.

(Just a side note: My high school sweetheart and friend became a minister, and I had gone to hear him preach recently. Members of his church came to greet me, and I mentioned that I was an old friend of the Reverend Smith. Until that moment, I had never stuttered in my life. To refer to such an old friend as the Reverend Anybody seems to have overwhelmed my brain and short-circuited my verbal abilities. It actually took a few tries to get it out. I can say it easily now, although I still can't help grinning when I do.)

Mistakes will happen. I still use the wrong name or pronoun on occasion, but then we all do that all the time anyway, don't we? I just treat it like any other slip of the tongue and keep going. I have found that no one has ever noticed. Anyone who is transitioning must understand (or simply remember) that ALL of us make mistakes in speech all the time. I don't take it personally. It is just a slip of the tongue and I treat it that way. ALL concerned seemed to become comfortable with it all when they saw our comfort.

Even Judy, our eleven year old daughter, has found a way to deal with the name change. Sally is Judy's "Daddy" and "he" at home, school, and among family and friends, and "Sally" and "she" in public. She occasionally makes a mistake and uses the "D word" in public, we treat it like any other slip of the tongue and have never received even a curious glance. This way works for us.

I found it helpful sometimes, to imagine Bob was just changing his name to "Sam" instead of "Sally" I found that it would be no easier to remember, but I was more comfortable in that case. I had to admit how hard it was at times, but both the new names and pronouns did really did get easier with practice. They became just words again.

To those of you making these changes and asking us to make them, too, please bear with us. This takes a lot of getting used to, and we need time and your patience to practice and get it right. Our occasional slips back to your old name and/or pronouns are just old habits, which die hard. With practice and patience, this will probably soon cease to be an issue. Good luck and best wishes to all!

SILENCE = DEATH
Tamara Alexander
(for Max)

I have been wedded in spirit to Max Beck, member of the Intersex Society of North America, for almost five years. We live in Atlanta, Georgia, with our three cats. When I am not writing papers I am busy raising our three cats, and the consciousness of Emory psychology undergraduates.

We met in college, the first day of the spring semester, junior year. Having had an earlier class in that room, I stayed on. She was the first to arrive. Our eyes met across an empty classroom; the neon signboard in my head lit up; something was forever changed. I would spend the next two years chasing down the mystery behind that moment.

We became friends. Dinners at each other's houses. Study groups. Movie marathons. We even had a date - candlelight and wine, out alone, glowing at each other across the table. And I told myself that I had been wrong, that she was straight. Hell, she even got married. I resolved to live with that.

It wasn't until April of the following year that I finally told her about the one and only love affair I'd ever had with a woman, and she responded in kind. I thought that this bit of history must have been what I'd been reading when we first met — not that she didn't have feelings for women, just that they had not been about me. How could I have known how wrong I would be?

I returned home to Georgia after graduation. I held her hand in the procession and reminded myself that this was where it ended. She was happily married, and I was adrift. We started a correspondence, ostensibly because she had missed out on having someone to talk to when she was figuring out her sexual orientation, and wanted to be that person for me. She was finally talking to me, after two years, about being a lesbian.

We were peeling the onion, one layer at a time. In my confusion, I reunited with my ex. It was only then that she wrote to tell me how involved she really had been, how deeply it hurt her to have missed our chance, how badly she really had wanted to be with me. I wrote back that I loved her. That I expected to live with the ache of that regret for the rest of my life.... I sent her Robert Frost's "The Road Not Taken," copying it out by hand on the back of the envelope, sitting on the floor of a bookstore. She left Harold.

We spoke at all hours of the day over the next two weeks. I called her at work. "I need to come see you." I had expected her excitement, joy, anticipation. She sighed. Her tone was ominous. "Okay," she said. "Come. We'll talk. There are some things you should know about me." "That sounds serious," I said. She agreed, "It is." My first thought was that she had cancer. My next thought was much closer to the mark.

The visit was to be two weeks later. The topic kept coming back; there were things that I should know about her. She didn't want to talk about them over the phone. Panic would break into her voice at the subject. "Why are you so afraid to tell me?" I asked. "Nothing could change the way I feel about you." "This could, " she said. "It's horrid." Eventually the strain of not talking about it won out, and she told me. By this time, I was already fairly certain what she was going to say.

"When I was born, the doctors couldn't tell whether I was a boy or a girl." She dictated the speech as if she'd told it many times before and all of the emotion had fallen right out of it. I finally heard the complete story of her college affair with a woman, who had said six words in bed that altered the entire course of Max's life: "Boy, Judy, you sure are weird." Max told me she knew then that she was a lesbian, but one who could not be with women because they would

102

know how her body was different. She married Harold because men were just less sensitive to the subtleties of women's anatomy.

My response was tears, "I can't believe you've been carrying this around by yourself your whole life." I hadn't been surprised; growing up in a house full of medical texts had acquainted me with intersexuality. I was not, as she had feared, horrified, repulsed, or anxious.

"What did you think," she asked me in the car as I was preparing to write this essay about loving her, "what did you expect my body to be like? "I thought it would be mysterious and wonderful," I told her. "And it was."

I went up to Philadelphia for four short days over her birthday in February. We attempted to cook, burned the butter, and collapsed in each others' arms on the floor. We left the house only to pick up take-out and Ben & Jerry's Wavy Gravy ice cream. Nonetheless, for the first two nights, she would not take off her boxer shorts. I could feel the wonder of her pressing against me through the flannel, but I was not allowed to touch. Although the rest of her body lay out before me to be charted, the triangle of flesh between her legs was a guarded region. She told me she couldn't lubricate because of the scar tissue, and because the surgeons had taken her labia to make a vaginal opening when she was fifteen. "Lots of women can't lubricate," I told her. "That's why they make feminine lubricants."

We decided to go shopping. In the feminine hygiene aisle, we compared the relative merits of Gyne-Moistrin and its competitors. When I looked up at Max, her eyes were wide and glazed. She was shaking. Her breath was irregular. I picked up the nearest product, sent her outside to wait, and paid at the register. We went home.

That night we slept downstairs in front of the fire. It was February 5, her 29th birthday. There was easily a foot of snow on the ground and it had all frozen over. Only her boxers still remained between us. Later that night she went upstairs to the bathroom, and when she slipped back under the covers, my hands slid from one end of her body to the another. The boxers were gone. I will never be able to recapture the magic of that moment. "Ohhh!" She was terrified, and I was aware of her fear and the cost of offering herself up to me in that moment. I have never wanted to pleasure someone, never wanted to offer my hands and my fingers to heal and to love and to delight, I have never been so awed by the feeling of touching as I was that night. I wanted to stroke and explore and learn and know every inch of her, the lines and crevasses from scars and healings, the tight cavern which held my fingers so tightly. She pulled me down on top of her and wrapped her arms around me and came, calling my name, sobbing against my shoulder. And I wept with her.

I wept for the loss of what she hadn't had and the lovers who hadn't reveled in the wonder of her body, wept for what I hadn't had before I held her in love, and I am weeping as I write this now.

It was a full year before she let me touch her that way again. A full year. We were still taking baby steps toward completely open lovemaking. Still peeling onions.

We moved to Atlanta in the summer of 1995. Broken by the stresses of new jobs, financial worries, lack of friends and supports, and a 1904 bungalow which we loved but could barely afford renovating, Max lapsed into a depression. She began to tell me that she was a monster and she just shouldn't be here. The day she did not go to work because she was planning to hang herself, I took her to the hospital. It was the hardest thing I have ever done in my life.

I had the unenviable task of surrendering the illusion that my unconditional love and acceptance were going to save her. No matter how much I loved her, no matter what I would give to heal her, I was not enough. I could not keep her safe. I could not erase thirty years of grief and doubt about her worth and her place in this world.

I was isolated from other people in ways I hadn't been before; no one knew her past medical history, and she was not ready for me to talk to anyone else about it. My friends from Philly called to check on me; they loved me and understood only that I was in agony because Max was depressed. They assured me that she would get better, that she would come home to me and the beautiful life we had created together. I was not certain she could ever recover from the damage that had been done.

I read her medical records over and over. Sorted through John Money's articles left from college psych classes. Read her journal, trying to understand. At night, I screamed my lungs out at the sheer futility of trying to help her. I had nightmares of surgeons wielding shiny scalpels, tying her down, and rearranging her body. I wept at work. I wept at home. I did endless battle with our mounting financial doom; the mortgage was late, the car unpaid, utilities coming due — all without her income. How would I ever keep things intact so that she had a life to return to when — if— she recovered?

I read her records, and I wondered, if this had happened to me, if my body had been desecrated and abused and held up in public life for the amusement of interns, would I have survived it even half as well as she had? Would I have had the courage to go on for thirty years with the memory of those rapes, my mother's shame and my own, and the lies of doctors?

I made promises to keep myself sane. I swore that I would not lose her. I swore that I would not allow this to happen to anyone else. I promised myself that if she slid off the face of this earth out of the exhaustion of fighting for her right to exist, I would not allow this to happen to any child like her. I would find out how and by whom this awful process was being perpetuated, and I would make it stop.

It took four months. Three hospitalizations. Persistent suicidal ideation and unwavering depression. She lost her job because she couldn't stop crying. I dragged her to monthly support group meetings in the gender community. I made her return calls to Cheryl Chase at ISNA. I pushed her to call the people Cheryl sent out to make contact with her. Each time, she would feel a little less alone, and a little more hopeful. And then the depression would creep back, telling her to give up. Telling her she would never be whole, would never be accepted, would never be anything but a shameful secret. As many times as I had learned in that first precious year together that love is an amazing healer, I had still to learn that sometimes shame and blatant evil can be stronger.

It is now almost a year since that last depression. It still creeps up on us from time to time. When she doesn't come home on time, I have to pace myself not to panic. I have to remind myself that not being home does not mean she has killed herself. But the danger is always there. It's only in the last few weeks that it feels less close, less powerful than myself. Less powerful than the sense of self I'm amazed and awed to watch her discover.

She has cut her hair, embraced butch, and found a good endocrinologist. We marched together in the parade at Gay Pride. I have come to believe myself a part of this community. I may not be transgendered, transsexual, or intersexed. I may have been fortunate enough to be born into a body that matches my sense of self and is accepted by society in its original form. But this is still my fight.

There is a popular slogan in the gay community that proclaims "silence = death." Her silence, and mine, almost meant her death. I am reminded of the words of the clergyman who recalled that during the Holocaust he did not speak because he was not a member of any of the groups being rounded up for execution. When they came for him, there was no one left to speak for him.

She is my partner, my love, the greatest gift life ever gave me. I choose to honor her decision to stay alive. I choose to speak on a daily basis. I honor her courage and her complexity. If she walks between the worlds set up by a gender-dichotomous society, then that is where my path leads as well.[6]

Coda

Max is now completely recovered from the depression, and has recently decided to transition to a male gender role. We feel strengthened by adversity, and look forward to the continued growth of our relationship. We are hoping to add a baby to our now-happy and secure family. Partners of intersexuals are welcome to contact me, through the editor, for mutual support.

CHALLENGE AND OPPORTUNITY
Anne Giles

I have a background in occupational therapy, working with emotionally disturbed children and adoption, but have been an at-home mom most of my life. I also led adoptive parent support groups for many years. My spouse, Diane, and I now host a monthly potluck in our home as a supportive experience for the trans community and their significant others.

The experience of dealing with any special circumstance has the potential for difficulties, but also possibility for many positive results. The Chinese character for crisis also means opportunity.

When my husband and I became adoptive parents of an autistic (severely emotionally disturbed) child who had lived at the residential school where I worked, most of the families in the school's parents' group could not understand why we would have taken on this "burden" and had dire predictions regarding the outcome. There was one couple, though, who told us, "You think you are only doing this for him, but you will get much more back from your relationship with him than you ever give."

Thirty-two years later, we know the truth of what they said. Because of our autistic son, we went on to adopt seven more "special needs" children after the birth of our two homemade sons. Korean, Vietnamese, Chinese-American and African-American, the children came to us with challenges including cerebral palsy, post-polio, learning and language disabilities, and emotional/behavioral difficulties due to their backgrounds. Their ages when they came to us ranged from three and one half to eighteen years old. Was it easy or always fun? No. It included hard work and frustration. There was also humor, and satisfaction, and love.

My life has been wonderfully enriched by the hundreds of people I have met in the adoptions and disabilities network, by the skills I gained, through the incredible variety of experiences we have had with our children, and most of all by the children themselves.

Although my husband's transgenderism is totally different from autism, my experience with it is in some ways similar, comprised of hurt and frustration and humor and love and an overall sense of enrichment.

I did not "choose" the transgender connection, but when I learned, two years into our marriage, that my husband liked to wear women's clothes, I chose to stay with him. Our lives were busy and his wearing women's underclothes was an issue that we put in the background, not talking or learning much about it but not being comfortable with it either. He thought it was a terrible thing; I did not like the hiding and secrecy nor the questions it made me ask about myself. What I did not know was that his attempts to suppress the behavior were the cause over the years of his growing rigidity, anger, depression, and need to be "perfect."

At the age of 57, when the distractions of children and eldercare were reduced and a year of "purging" (putting aside all feminine items) had only intensified his depression, Dick was finally ready to address his crossdressing — with a push from me in my insistence that he accept it as a part of himself and not something that was awful.

He "outed" himself as a crossdresser to our family and community, and found amazing acceptance by almost everyone. Our home-made son's reaction was "Is that all," and although some of our other adult children had concerns, they all worked their way through them. His 82-year-old mother said "Welcome" when told, and soon was advising him that "You need a red blouse to go with your new vest."

When Diane, as Dick's femme self, went out and about there

were occasional stares or double-takes, but no one was rude and most reactions varied from polite to outright friendly. Clerks gave good service, and waiters saying "Ma'am" thrilled Diane. I usually accompanied Diane and our fears and embarrassments turned to relief. I'm sure some who saw Diane went home and said,"Maude, do you know what I saw!", but we began starting our forays into the world with a smile and the refrain "Let's go make someone's day.

During that first year Dick was able to acknowledge that he had always wanted to be a woman and realized that he is transgendered, perhaps transsexual. Assisting him in his journey toward full-time living as Diane, the woman that he was meant to be, was not easy for me, but it was far better than the pain of the previous years. The fact that we had a solid marriage built on mutual respect and concern for each other was crucial: I supported and helped Diane even while grieving the loss of my "husband"; Diane held back and waited until I was emotionally ready for each step of the process.

Some of our sons and daughters had an even harder time working through accepting dad as a woman rather than just a crossdresser. Again, it seemed easiest for our homemade sons, but by the end of the first year all but one daughter had come to terms with it and ranged from welcoming to comfortable to accepting. As one son who lives at a distance, and had worried about visiting home because of the change, said on his first visit, "Oh, it's still just dad." Most of our children still call Diane "dad," which does cause some interesting - and funny— situations, such as our African-American daughter cheerily calling to the white woman ahead of her, "Hey, DAD!"

Our grandchildren, as with most pre-teen children, seem to just accept it without much concern, and were satisfied with simple answers: "Why does grandpa wear dresses?" "Because she likes to." "Oh."

Diane has found acceptance as a full-time woman. She started the new semester of her junior college math classes with "I know you expected Dick Giles. Would you believe I am his identical twin sister, Diane? I am transgendered. If you want to know more, come see me in my office, but now let's do math." It was Diane's happiest and best year of teaching.

Our local newspaper picked up the story and ran an understanding article which went out nationwide on AP wire. Yet even with a listed phone number we never had any harassing calls. Diane looks great and a couple of years practicing her makeup, hair styling and clothes selection have helped, but at six feet in height and with sixty years of male hormones, she still does not always "pass." She would dearly love always to be seen as the woman that she knows she is, but she consoles herself that when she does not "pass," she is doing outreach for the trans community. But "pass" or not, she and I shop, travel, socialize and live our normal lives without difficulty.

As in parenting a "special" child, being married to a "special" spouse has at times been difficult, but increasingly the benefits have almost entirely taken over. I enjoy my newfound openness to the diverse and very enjoyable group of trans people we have met and have made many new friends. Diane's transformation has provided me with an opportunity for self-examination, growth and learning, and has deepened and improved our relationship. She is so much happier — gender euphoria she calls it — and that happiness is reflected in our lives. I thought I was sacrificing to make Diane a fulfilled person, but in truth I, too, have benefited greatly.

P.S. In case you are wondering, our autistic son really likes Diane.

~~~~~~~~~~

Benjamin Franklin is reported to have said that all of mankind is divided into three classes: Those that are immovable, those that are movable, and those that move. I say: Let us be the movers and focus on those who are movable. (Mary Boenke)

GROWTH AND LOVE
Samantha Star Straf

I am a 33-year-old network analyst from central Illinois. Some of the terms that I use to describe myself are: bisexual, polyamorous, Unitarian-Universalist, pagan, science fiction fan, cat lover, friend.

I have grown a lot in the last three years, my partner even more so; sometimes it is good to look back and see that progress. My partner, Pooch, and I had been close friends for almost ten years before we started dating three years ago.

He had come to terms with his cross dressing and had decided that next time he got involved with someone he would tell them up front, so on our second date I was handed a stack of photos and told "I want to share something special about myself with you." My first reaction was to wonder who his girlfriend was, then I realized the similarity and with a sigh of relief said "This is you." I was the first person outside the transgender community ever to know about Andrea. I would like to share a few of our learning experiences, compromises that we have made, and how those have evolved and changed.

My first concern was the fact that Andrea was "in the closet." I had gone through the coming out process as a bisexual and realized that it is very hard for me to live with a secret, so the first compromise we made was that she would have to come out more than she was. I wanted permission to tell my friends and not to have to watch what I say. Together we have brought Andrea out of the closet (leaving much more room for her clothes <grin>), starting by slowly telling Pooch's best friends. Luckily almost all the reactions have been loving and positive.

Some family members either do not know or do not want to talk about it but pretty much everyone else knows. This puts me at ease since I have trouble remembering who knows and who does not know a secret. In the last year we have both been doing some community education and outreach, speaking at the Unitarian Universalist Church for their Welcoming Congregation workshops. I also have spoken out in my psychology classes.

The next issue we struggled with was time. For a while there was such excitement at having an accepting partner that there was much more Andrea time than Pooch time. Considering that we lived half a continent apart, that made for some struggles. We decided to make sure there was equal time scheduled, that for every Andrea visit there was also a Pooch visit. One trick I learned from a significant others email list was to have Pink/Blue days. When I put an event on the calendar I have the right to mark it either Pink (I want Andrea at this event) or Blue (I want Pooch at this event). If it doesn't have a color then it doesn't matter to me which presentation he makes.

Another time-related problem was the time it takes for Andrea to get ready. I am not one to fuss with makeup and hair so having to wait for her bothered me. We both compromised on this one. With more practice and electrolysis her preparation time was shortened and I have learned both to remind her when to start and to have a book to read. On another occasion when she was having a bad hair day, I offered to get a carry-in breakfast if she would pay for it, so we could make the meeting I wanted to attend. She agreed and we both got what we needed. We have learned to be specific on needs versus wants, to let the other know what is important, and to be open to creative solutions.

When I first found out about Andrea I read all the books I could find about transgenderism, got on many e-mail lists, and submerged myself in information. One of my fears was that many transsexuals start as cross-dressers and later decide to transition. I did not think I could handle that. Even though Pooch said he was definitely a cross dresser I still had fears. I decided that a "I will promise to be your friend but I can not promise to be your partner if you decide to tran-

112

sition" statement would make me feel much more comfortable. Pooch has been very good about checking with me for any steps that might be intimidating for me.

Before he started electrolysis he dug out all the old photos of him with beard and we talked about what I would miss if he got electrolysis. He has looked into hair loss options and we compromised on external solutions instead of internal drugs, at least until there is more research on side effects.

Since then I have decided that since I love this person down to the marrow of my bones, I would be able to stay through any transition should his gender identification change.

Sexuality is the final ground that I want to tread today. Although I am bisexual, Andrea is not the femme type of woman that I would be involved with. It took some time for me to feel comfortable with Andrea in the bedroom, but taking small steps and talking about comfort levels was very useful. I took lots of advice from many significant others, about Andrea wearing Pooch's cologne, having some foreplay with Andrea but then switching to Pooch when things got sexual. Also, loving a cross-dressed woman is much different than being intimate with a genetic or post-op woman; the "parts" just do not fit with the image. It took me some time to throw out my assumptions about what sexuality was and the differences between being with men and being with women. I am learning to make love to the person, not the gender.

Our journey has been a fairly easy one, made much easier by lots of information and communication. Learning how to talk and compromise about transgender issues has made all aspects of our relationship healthier and stronger. We have learned not only about each other but about ourselves. I hope that others can also experience such a rich and joyous journey.

PART IV

CRUCIAL OTHERS

LOVE YOU, DADDY, NO MATTER WHAT
Emma Rowe

My name is Emma and I am fifteen years old. I have a younger brother, Alex, who is nine. I am in year eleven at school (my last year). In the future I am hoping to do a course at college, and then, hopefully, become an infant school teacher or a nursery nurse.

Dear Mary,

I am a 15 year old girl from England. A few months ago my Father came out to us as a transsexual. To say we were surprised would be an understatement. I am coping generally fairly well, but I have problems with the thought of losing my father. I have told one or two close friends including my boyfriend and they have no problem with it, but all the same it is causing me a fair deal of worry. I have started to receive counselling at school, but it isn't really helping much as the counsellor doesn't have much experience of this matter.

A couple of weeks ago we had a family crisis during which it became obvious that we were having problems. My dad promptly decided to stop his treatment because he could see how much we were hurting and he loves us so much that he couldn't carry on doing this to us. The next day, while he was at work, mum and I talked over what we would do, and decided that my dad should carry on with the treatment or it would tear him apart.

Just before I talked to mum, I spent quite some time thinking, myself, and composed this letter to him. If you think it is suitable for inclusion in your book then please use it. I am enclosing it in this e-mail.

Yours,
Emma Rowe.

117

Dear Dad:

I have thought a great deal about it all and I want to tell you, in this letter, what I find hard to say to your face.

I am trying hard to understand what you are going through. I suppose I could never understand completely, but I know for a fact what you must do, what you need to do. It will be very hard for me, but I think I may be able to come to terms with this (I am speaking on behalf of myself. Mum and I haven't talked properly as of yet.)

I am going to find it very hard to face you; it will be very difficult with you not being my dad. I love mum dearly, but I suppose you could say I'm a daddys girl. I have decided you should carry on with the treatment, because I know how important this is to you, and I want what is best for you. I will be able to get through this, with your love and support and with the help of family, friends and counsellors, but if you stopped treatment altogether — will you get through?

You may be able to get help, but the feeling is always going to be there, do you want to go on living a lie? I believe you and I both know the answer.

I would also have to carry the guilt of not letting you have what you want, what you need. And as you said before, once a transsexual always a transsexual. All I want is for you to be happy, and seeing you happy, will make me happy.

Please, will you get me professional help to get me through this.?

Love you always,
Emma

MY NEW GRANDDAUGHTER
Clela Fuller Morgan

I raised four children, spent time as a missionary, and worked as a nurse. I have retired to Camron, Missouri where I enjoy researching and writing for the local paper about the historical houses in the area.

I used to have eight grandsons and two granddaughters and now have seven grandsons and three granddaughters; the most recent is the oldest. That might be difficult to explain, but not after you have met Danielle.

It has been a little more than a year since Evelyn told me that her 15-year-old son, Daniel, had revealed to her that he believed he was really a girl. Almost immediately I said, "He has always been a girl!"

You see, I have many memories of this special child. I remember the small boy of about three years who often sat on the arm of the couch combing and arranging his mother's long and curly hair. (He was still styling her hair years later.) That small boy liked to play with dolls and he saw some kind of value in a dismembered Barbie doll among the toys that I kept for visiting children. On his ninth birthday, his wish was for a doll with long hair and a pony with a long mane — and the family fulfilled his wish. Several times he had me help him make clothes for his doll. He would pick out some material from the scrap box and together we would fashion clothes. His choice of cloth was always the bright shiny pieces.

In kindergarten, when he was getting settled in a new school, I asked how he liked it. He said, "It's beautiful! The colors are so pretty." I didn't understand that statement until I had an occasion to pick him up from school. Every schoolroom door around the big court was painted a different color — pink, purple, green, blue, yellow — so it was very colorful. He always described textures as well as colors whenever it was appropriate.

He never played any sports except when he was involved in acrobatic classes, which seemed to fit him naturally. He did exceptionally well with that.

This little grandson was extremely loving. I always got a big hug when he came to visit, another when he left, and usually a time or two during the stay. He was also very sensitive to other people's feelings. He could tell when someone was not feeling well or was angry or uncomfortable.

At an age when most little boys were finding their friends from among the boys, his friends were girls. When he had a chance to take two or three friends on an outing on his birthday, he always picked girls, and this pattern of having girls for his close friends continued through junior high school.

Daniel was always close to his mother in ways that you would not expect of a son. They appeared to have such fun together. When he became old enough to be aware of his mother's clothes, he would advise her what to wear, and later she always took him along to pick out new clothes for her wardrobe. Two years ago his mother and I helped to host a bridal shower for a friend. Her son, then thirteen years old, arranged her hair. He used a small chignon of curls on the back of her head and, with a ribbon, blended it in with her own curls. The style was perfect with the flower print and lace of her dress. She was pretty as a picture, and Daniel appreciated and praised her beauty profusely.

He was the one in the family who would get the urge to clean and straighten the house, and would get after his brothers to put things away. As he started to think about his life work, he chose interior decorating. At one time I sent him a subscription to an interior decorating magazine, and I knew he liked to visit model homes to look at the furnishings.

Those of us close to this special child recognized that he was different, but had no clue as to the cause. He was very animated as he talked, with unusual movements of his hands and body. As I

120

watched him walk, I sometimes thought, "Can't he walk like a boy? Doesn't he know he walks like a girl?" He knew, because his school-mates teased him about his walk, and I know now that he couldn't do anything about it. Now we see those same movements and animation and feminine gait as perfect for a teenage girl.

The age at which Danielle made this drastic change was unusual, for more often it is made much later in life. It wasn't a sudden idea, for Evelyn knew some months before the announcement that Daniel was emotionally upset. Some have wondered if a teenager of sixteen years should be making this important decision. Consider this question: At what pont in life did you make the "decision" to be male or female?

...What I think is commendable is that Evelyn immediately sought professional advice to assist Danielle to make the transition in the way that was best for her. This led to psychological testing, electrolysis, and hormone therapy — treatments which were uncomfortable and sometimes painful for Danielle. The fact that her brothers, cousins, aunts and uncles on both sides of her family were supportive, with one or two exceptions, is also commendable.

Some who have had qualms about getting acquainted with Danielle have had their doubts immediately swept away when they meet the beautiful, vivacious, out-going young lady....I am so pleased to see her blossom scholastically and socially and her excitement about life is contagious. She has courageously faced the necessary difficulties and recognizes that the road ahead won't be easy, but she is up to it. Life sometimes uses strange ways to teach us tolerance and understanding of persons who have problems different from our own. How fortunate we are to be able to learn this lesson from Danielle![7]

A DOUBLE-SPECIAL BROTHER
Victoria Moon*

I am a graduate student studying bilingual special education, planning to teach elementary children. I like the outdoors, traveling, hiking, backpacking, biking, making clothes and jewelry. I am a humanist, a member of both the local PFLAG chapter and a transgender community group, and an activist for human rights, environment, and educational rights. My friends have been very supportive and I now tell anyone who asks — I have two brothers!

It's 2:08 am and here I sit to write a story about my life and my brother. Who am I? Well, I am a reflection of everyone I have ever been in contact with, but for the purposes of this book I am a proud sister of a female-to-male transgendered individual. Eight years my senior, my former sister was a strong female figure given a lot of parental responsibilities. My mother left my father when I was three years old, deciding to raise her three kids on her own.

Mikeal, my brother (former sister) and the oldest, was left to watch us while mom was at school or work. He and I have always had a special relationship. He is Deaf, so he relied on me to be his ears when we were in public. He had an amazing ability for reading my lips, so whenever he wanted to know what others were saying he would ask me. Often I spoke to him using no voice; it was cool. However, now we use American Sign Language, which he learned after his high school graduation.

Since Mikeal's early years he had boyish tendencies and interests. He hated dolls and never wore dresses. He loved cars and

122

sports. My mom was pretty supportive, thinking of him as a tomboy who would grow out of it. My Dad rejected him because of the communication breakdown. I remember one time when my brother and I were at the playground. The playground lady asked who the cute boy was with me and I told her that's not a boy, that's my sister! On the way home my brother asked me what we said and I told him. He loved it. In fact, he purposely bought boy clothes and tried to suppress his bust.

In the mid '80's, Mikeal went off to college and found himself in the punk scene. There he could hide his femininity and be accepted as "cool." He also came to terms with his attraction to women. When he told me he was a lesbian, I shrugged and said I knew. He couldn't believe how understanding I was, but I love my brother and neither his gender nor his sexual orientation will ever change that.

He was an important figure for me, growing up. He protected me from my other brother and my father. For many years Mikeal was considered a "butch lesbian." I know now he wasn't "butch" at all; he was a straight man trapped in a woman's body. As he went through lesbian relationships he realized his true identity. Women would say, "you're not gay," "you're different," or "you're not like other women." Finally, in his last lesbian relationship, his girlfriend brought up the notion that he might be transgendered. He thought, "Wow! Maybe that's why things are so hard for me in the lesbian community. Yeah, I do feel like a guy!" So, he began to research it a little bit.

That's when he ran into an old friend from high school. She was very supportive and actually was attracted to my brother. They began a long-distance relationship for a while. Now they live in the same town, but it is very difficult. Mikeal is a pre-op so he has difficulty passing, especially with the rising lesbian/butch population and acceptance in town. So his girlfriend often gets mislabeled as a lesbian. This upsets her because she loves my brother as a man. One day, after his identity is legally changed, they would like to settle and have a family.

Probably the biggest challenge Mikeal faces is that he is Deaf.

The Deaf community can be pretty closed-minded, so he constantly fears rejection. He works closely with the Deaf community as an historian of the language and culture. He is an educator in this community and highly respected. Because his girlfriend has already been mislabeled as a lesbian, they are unable to be together and present as a couple in the Deaf community. Really, it's horrible for them. Plus, to get the support he needs in order to go through this change he needs an interpreter. It's ironic and very difficult, because he trained most of those same interpreters! They are thinking of moving because they are known and misunderstood by too many people there.

Recently, Mikeal and his girlfriend came to visit me and I introduced them to other transgendered individuals. It was the first time he ever had face-to-face contact with another FtM. It was wonderful! It brought a sense of hope to both of them. I am hoping that they will relocate here, where there are more understanding people, because here they could make a fresh start.

As I think back, when my brother first told me the news of his decision to become a man, I wasn't too shocked. I cried, though. I thought of my family and how they wouldn't accept him. I did feel betrayed and tricked for all those years of identifying with HER. I had looked up to her as an empowered woman who didn't need to act feminine to be a woman. She broke all the rules and shocked people; she was strong and protective. I had thought of him as androgynous. This raises an interesting question about what gender really is. Looking back, I realize how my now-brother has shaped my view. I believe that we should each strive to balance gender within us. We should celebrate our femininity as well as our masculinity. Although I am quite feminine-looking, I embrace my masculine side.

My boyfriend has been especially supportive and helpful in correcting my pronouns and also introduced me to an amazing MtF woman. Patricia and I have had long discussions and she connected me with PFLAG. At PFLAG, I met a wonderful mother of an FtM, who has taught me to discuss our own situation more fully with my own mother.

My family has the general attitude that they will believe it when they see it. It sort of reminds me of their attitude when my brother changed his name back in his early twenties. He decided to go by his more androgynous-sounding middle name. At first my family didn't take him seriously and thought it was a phase. However, my brother would get really offended if they referred to him by his old name. Now, as time has passed, almost everyone calls him by his middle name except my father.

We have a very strange relationship with my father. Since his remarriage eighteen years ago, he has had difficulty including us in his life. He truly believes that we are all too busy in our own lives to make it happen. He doesn't know about Mikael's plans; I think he might have a clue, but denies it. My other biological brother has mixed feelings but I think he'll come around. Everyone in the family still communicates with Mikael.

I have been in close contact with my mother. I tell her about the groups I attend and encourage her to seek support. She is in some denial but doesn't correct me when I refer to my brother as a "he" in conversation, so I am happy. My mom's husband is on the same wave length as my mom. They are proud people and that prevents them from seeking support. My mom once told me that my brother is a part of her and that she loves him very much, so she would not shut him out. However, my mom still refers to my brother as a "she."

For many years Mikeal was a male basher who taught me to be wary of men and their sexual intentions. For that I am thankful, but I do struggle to trust men and let myself go. When my brother came out to me my first question was, "Why do you want to be a man; you hate men!"

He explained, with feeling, that he had bashed men because he was jealous. All his life he has walked in the shadows of men, only to be seen as a woman! He is cursed with large breasts which still torture him every day of his life. One day, they will be gone and we will certainly celebrate!

SHE'LL ALWAYS BE MY FATHER
Debbie McKellar Donaldson

I am 29, and work long hours as a cashier. I enjoy bicycling, sewing, and playing with my dog.

When I was growing up, there were good times and conflicts as in any other family I knew. We were living the average middle-class American life and everything seemed fine to me. It was not until I was nine years old that I was told about our family secret. My father was a cross-dresser and had been for all of my life. This admission shocked me, of course, but I was really too young to understand what was going on. Over the next four or five years the cross-dressing continued with my knowledge. However, our encounters at home, when he was dressed, were infrequent enough that I was able to block out the feeling that my father was a freak.

Things changed, however, when I was thirteen or fourteen years old. He actually started wearing these clothes in front of me on a regular basis! It became routine. When he came home from work he would check the mail and proceed to go change. Other than the clothes, the evening went on as always. During my teen years, I spent a lot of time in my room to get away. I also kept very busy with school, a job, and my friends. I did anything I could to distance myself from the "freak." Needless to say, there was a lot of discord in the house and animosity between us.

Things finally came to a head when I was eighteen. I found my own place and moved out. Things were tough, but there was no way that I was going back. Shortly thereafter, my parents separated and filed for divorce. In a period of approximately seven or eight months my father had effectively erased his family from his life.

Over the next two years or so, I would occasionally visit my father and share small talk to catch up. A close friend of mine likened

126

these visits to business meetings because of our demeanor. Over time, however, I began to notice changes. His hair was getting longer and he seemed to be developing — dare I say it — breasts? Finally, my father put me out of my questioning misery and gave me a letter. This was his way of coming out of the closet so he could live his life, publicly, as a woman. The letter explained the steps that he would be taking: a name change, changing the sex on the drivers license, and everything else that goes with becoming a new person. When I read that letter I felt as though I would fall over. This piece of paper was telling me that my father was essentially dead. After this revelation, I saw my father even less than ever.

Suddenly, about three years ago, I grew up. Visits became more frequent and conversations were longer and more enlightening.

Now, I am twenty-eight years old. I am proud of who my father has become and the person that she is. She is not ashamed of her identity and does a lot of work in the community. She is also a major force in the transgender community. She is working nationally and internationally to help make things better for other people who are having trouble adjusting to their identity.

I still have problems getting my pronouns straight and on occasion I still accidently call her Dad in public. She is patient, though, and tells me that it will just take time. She tells me that she is thankful that we are talking because there are kids that sometimes turn completely away from their parents. Sometimes I space my visits apart, but I could never lose complete contact. After all, deep down inside is the person who raised me. She is still my father.

* * * *

N.B. This was written by the daughter and only child of Dee McKellar just days before Dee's sudden death from a heart attack September 6, 1997 (See In Memory)

FAMILY
Denny M.

My early years were dominated by fear; it has taken many years and much help to rewrite my family's "script" and to start living my own truth. I now live a life with increasing love, joy, gratitude, and purpose. I am in a partnership with a man — but my friend, Rebecca, is a very important part of my life. In many ways, she made my life with Will possible.

When I came out as a gay man five years ago, I dreamed of developing a relationship with that "special man." I never dreamed that the greater gift of coming out would be my friendship with a very special woman, Rebecca. Rebecca is special because of her many gifts, and she is special to me for many other reasons. Unfortunately, most people would say that Rebecca is "special" solely because she is a "woman born man." Funny, but today I almost never see that distinction.

Believe me, it wasn't always this way! I met Rebecca in a 12-step recovery program for gays and lesbians. I am ashamed to say that when I first saw her that night, my stomach really turned. Her mere presence frightened me. Here was this big bruiser of a person, with few clues to tell me what sex s/he was, save breasts (were they real?) and a blond wig that didn't look the least bit natural. For the first month, I avoided her gaze— and stared at her when she wasn't looking.

They say in Program that your Higher Power has a wicked sense of humor. They also say that God gives you just the "opportunities for growth" you need. So guess who asked me to be her sponsor one meeting?

To help me better understand her and make my decision, Rebecca shared with me parts of her story, told via an allegorical autobiography. I have since learned the real details, and they are even more amazing.

Rebecca was born with "indeterminate sex." For the first seven years of her life, she was raised as a girl. Of course, our male-dominated society thought anyone having anything even remotely resembling a penis must be a man. So one day Rebecca's clothes and dolls were burned— before her eyes— her hair was cut, and presto... she was now "Jackie!"

I still have difficulty piecing together details of the next sixteen years of her life. Attempts to force her "true" gender on her during these years include hormone shots, being shipped off to boarding school, commitment to psychiatric institutions and numerous hospitalizations. In her pain, Rebecca turned to juvenile delinquency, violence and alcoholism. She was hospitalized or jailed on more than one occasion. These years also include distinguished service in Vietnam, married life, and fathering two wonderful children.

I do not know and cannot judge Rebecca's parents or family for their initial or subsequent decisions around Janice. I do know that when she decided to divorce her wife and start the transition process, her family disowned her. She was considered dead to them until only a few years ago. Her father spurned her, even to the time of his death.

Needless to say, I was, and still am, overwhelmed by Rebecca's courage and the power of her spirit. After all she has been through, I am amazed she is still walking around this planet—in a sane state! It has been a gratifying honor to serve as her sponsor. It has been an even greater learning lesson and joy to be her friend.

Over the last five years, I have passed through a number of "growth opportunities" learning to love a transgendered person. The first challenge was facing my transphobia head on. In the early days, I was afraid of what people would think of me for being with her. I used to stare around furtively in public places like restaurants, wondering if anyone was watching us. It took me a long time to use the right pronouns. At first, it had to be a very conscious activity. I remember one time when we were at a party. Tired, and with a drink or two under my belt, I referred to her as "he" more than once. The next day Rebecca called me and rightfully expressed her anger and hurt.

I wish I could say that that was the extent of my "travels in transphobia." But I also remember at another point in our relationship conspiring with more than one "woman born woman" to find ways to make Rebecca "look more feminine." (Thankfully, I never tried to foist any of these plans on her.) Until recently, I felt compelled to "warn" people who didn't know Rebecca "what" she was. This is what I am aware of and own. I'm sure there were other "transgressions" I made (and may still be making) during my growth process.

I have been asked how I overcame my transphobia. The truest answer I can come up with is that I didn't do anything. *Learning to love Rebecca taught me how to love.*

Rebecca has taught me the absolute truth of the kindergarten lesson, "don't judge a book by its cover." In addition to her courage and strength, Rebecca is bright (very, very bright!), funny, and consistently supportive in a very non-direct way. I now have that special man in my life, but not having been in a relationship for most of my life, I often struggle with the challenges it brings. Rebecca offers her experience with relationships (from both sides of the fence!) in a quiet way which never upsets me. She just asks me a quiet question or provides a little vignette that usually makes everything clear— even if I end up seeing my own fears and stubborn ego in the process! If it hadn't been for Rebecca's quiet counsel, Will and I might have been history a long time ago.

Rebecca is amazingly well-read and knowledgeable on a host of subjects. She is also helpful on "feminine things" such as computer hardware, electronics and aviation (smile). My discussions with her are rarely dull and always instructive — practically, intellectually and spiritually. *And I might have lost all this*, just because I couldn't accept her supposed spot on a fixed gender scale.

When I came to love Rebecca the person, her gender —past or present— became irrelevant. When I learned to cherish our relationship, I stopped worrying about what others thought about it. And when my thoughts stopped moving outward, I grew inward in my ability to love. This is undoubtedly the greatest gift I have received from knowing Rebecca.

Of course, our relationship has transformed both of us. My sponsorship gave Rebecca one person who (gradually) accepted and loved her totally for who she was. In the early years, I worked hard to help Rebecca recognize and fight the negative thoughts she took on from all those cruel people in her life. (Our first lesson was "I have a right to be on this planet because God placed me here.") My sponsorship and friendship has always emphasized the personal worth of both of us. And as Rebecca makes the small (and significant) changes in her life which are testimony to that worth, I have been there with suggestions, support and celebration for her growth.

Rebecca is not just my sponsoree, or my best friend. She is my family.

~~~~~~~~~~~

"Often I feel that the directions the tranz can take are limited too much. The roles we try to achieve are set by the very oppressor that cannot tolerate us. Confusion becomes the epitaph of so many of us. The journey should always remain a journey of self, not only of gender." (Macaylla Law)

ACCEPTANCE
Elizabeth Vickery

I graduated from Olivet College, married, have two daughters, and was widowed at age 36. I retired from Michigan Bell, married a second time at age 65 and was widowed again at age 79. A woman's club, poets society, aerobics and line dancing classes keep me active. I have five grandchildren and five great-grandchildren.

My grandson used to be my granddaughter. It is at his suggestion that, at age 82, I write about my acceptance of the problems, developments, and changes of the beautiful baby whom I saw only minutes after she was born.

Acceptance can begin early in life. I was about sixteen when my mother brought home Radclyffe Hall's *The Well of Loneliness* for me to read. I had seen the picture of her in the Literary Digest and had tried to figure out if she was a man or a woman. My reaction to the book was sympathy for all the suffering the girl had endured. I thought her novel must have been at least somewhat autobiograhical. My mother and I discussed her problems and feelings just as we had discussed *Candide* after I read that book.

Over the years I had talked to my aunt (my mother's sister), also, about all sorts of things. My mother's approach was mainly academic. My aunt's approach was more "down to earth." Between them, I learned a lot about understanding people, male and female.

Acceptance comes more easily when taught early. It also comes from being aware of the problems, changes and happenings over the years to someone you love — to children or grandchildren, for instance. It can be handed down from generation to generation. My mother was born in 1888. I was born in 1915, my daughter in 1942, and my grandon in 1960. When my grandson first came out to her mother, her response was, "Aren't you the person I loved five minutes ago before I knew you were gay?" I was very proud of her for that.

Several years ago my granddaughter, which she was at that time, asked me to go with her to a gay bar. I was probably the only straight person there. We danced together as we always had around home. I liked the women who were her particular friends. I still correspond with one of them once or twice a year.

Humor can be a great help in acceptance, the humor of both people. When my grandson came to visit, sporting a beard, for a day or two it was a little strange, but the personality and voice were very familiar. Two incidents made it much easier. I ran into friends at a restaurant and introduced my grandson. When we got outdoors, he said with a big grin, "Congratulations, Grandma!" "What for?" He replied, "You only called me 'she' twice."

We were in a meat market and the lady waiting on him turned to me as if to say she'd be right with me and I said, "I'm with her". She looked at my grandson with an odd look, clearly meaning "Is that old lady wacko? Can't she see you're a man?" He and I managed to keep our faces straight until we got outside, where we became convulsed with laughter. It was especially therapeutic to us both because we both could see the humor in the situation and the knowing look she gave him. Acceptance can be easy and/or difficult, but as my mother used to say, "You can't help people by turning your back on them." You can learn to understand, as well as to love, them.

MY BROTHER'S KEEPER?
Christopher Campbell*

I am in my forties, most recently lived in New Zealand, am a graphic designer and teacher, now working as a computer consultant in my own business in England. My younger brother, who was born intersexed and raised as a girl, was always a male. Because of a disabling accident, he needs to rely on a wheel chair for mobility. He became a specialist in children's mental health problems, transitioned back to male, and lives with his partner and me who share responsibility for his care.

Once, long ago. I became aware that a friend of mine, someone I had known through my boyhood and on into adult life, was gay. He didn't make a big deal of it because when the matter was aired, the climate of public opinion was turning, thanks in part, to a repeal of the draconian law which condemned untold thousands of gay people to a life of subterfuge or punishment as a criminal because of their sexuality. My reaction to his news was equally low-key since, within my own family, there were examples of both the broad brush of sexuality and the continuum of gender identity, the latter represented in the person of my brother.

I grew up in East Africa, a "child of Empire" so to speak, and saw more in my years there than most people see in their lifetimes. At an early age, I was aware of the rich tapestry of life on this planet. A brother who, despite his birth certificate proclaiming him to be of female gender, resolutely asserted that he was male, was a vital part of this tapestry. As I write this, my brother is continuing to live his life as a man who also happens to use a wheelchair. (I prefer this description of him, since he has so minimized his disability that it no longer forms part of my concept of him.)

It was not always thus. His use of a wheelchair was imposed by his involvement in a serious accident whilst he was at university. Driving back to college after a day of sailing, his car was hit from behind, pushed off the road and crashed down hill, causing irreparable spinal damage. Before that, he was strong and athletic, as fiercely independent as he is now, and well on the way to completing his transition — a journey that has taken him from a "female" child to a man. The child whose gender isn't sufficiently definitive fails to satisfy the demands of a society pre-occupied with a skewed perception of gender that permits only a bi-polar model. Those who fall outside this ring-fence have to be remodelled to fit, however loose the final garment proves to be.

In my brother's case, the "female" shell-suit never fit. He rebelled from his earliest days, his body language an instinctive manifestation of the male that still lived and flourished within him. He soon began to articulate his disdain for the female name that was chosen to match his perceived gender, refusing to answer to it. My brother now emerged from the shadows, to cause havoc in the tidy lines of infant school, where children get an early taste of the gender divide. He confused the narrow concepts of doting aunts who fussed around this little "girl" with his boyish way of brushing them aside.

Secure in my own male gender identity, I wondered at this tiny rebel who fought so hard for his. Despite the name he was given, the clothes he was expected to wear, the echoes of female pronouns that accompanied any reference to him, I found it difficult to see him as anything other than the boy he knew himself to be. We shared boyish things, such as boys' secrets and fears. I went to boarding school, but my brother stayed at home, refusing to even consider the possibility of being in close proximity to girls for twenty-four hours a day. The six hours in a mixed day school were quite enough for him. Even then he would come home, muddied and bloodied as boys do, but sometimes the wounds were those of a fledgling gender warrior whose patience with the teasing he received because of his "tomboy" ways had reached breaking point. Sometimes, I was there to comfort him; others times I wasn't and I can only guess at the years of silent torment he endured.

Adolescence brought even greater problems. My regard for him and my acceptance of his masculine identity wasn't so blinkered as to blind me to the prospects for his future, when (as I thought), his body would respond in complete contradiction to self-concepts of his gender. I feared for him and the way in which I thought his identity would be compromised by the onslaught of puberty. I was unaware, at this stage, of the thousands of transsexual youngsters who endured the trauma of a body that, day by day, turns the knife of gender dysphoria until the need for transition becomes an unstoppable force. In later years, I grew to know many transpeople and developed a deep respect for their courage and tenacity in a world that frequently consigns all women to the rank of second-class citizens, but reserves a special kind of distaste for men born to look like "women" or "men" who declare that they are, in reality, female.

My brother grew and confounded us all. The female model of puberty barely touched him, which in itself, was a two-edged sword. His body never followed the blue print of his birth certificate, no embarrassment of breasts and monthly cycle, but he paid a price for that small victory. The accepted tomboy of the junior school was metamorphosing into a less-acceptable masculine "girl", who was entirely out-of-place in the secondary school where gender roles and identity are so fiercely reinforced by puberty. The bloodied nose of his early years' battles was replaced by wounds that ran far deeper. His voice, always lower than his female peer-group, finally broke altogether when he was fourteen and shone a spotlight on him that pursued him to university. The freedom he craved and expected to open up for him in the relative anonymity of college was still elusive and it soon became evident that full transition was the only route to survival. Our family was generally supportive, since so many of them had born witness to his life-long struggle, but others, further removed from the inner circle, regarded his decision with a mixture of disbelief and scepticism.

The process of transition involved plans to boost my brother's male hormone levels followed by genital surgery. No part of this process is easy, on the mind or the body. Maybe in an ideal world, those who would tread the middle path of gender will be allowed to do so without fear. This third gender would be as accepted then as the bi-polar model is now. For those like my brother, who had lived every day of his life in the no-man's-land of androgyny and its consequences, a life spent on this middle path was a prospect that horrified him.

Maybe mere mortals such as we should never presume to plan too far ahead. Despite the hard work that had gone into my brother's reaching the point at which he and his immediate friends and family were prepared for him to transition, a serious accident and the need to re-plan his life around disability transcended every other consideration. Fortunately, this particular young man had been well-trained in the arena that society constructs for transpeople. He is tough, he is a fighter and he now used his tenacity to fight his way out of the latest prison to hold him. He returned to college and eventually graduated — with honours. The question of transition was aired again. The delay had only served to reinforce his certainty that he must take this step. Life as a disabled man didn't have much to commend it, but, for him, it beat the hell out of attempting to live as a disabled androgyne.

The effects of the hormone therapy were rapid. It was as if his body had been waiting, impatiently for the catalyst it needed to flourish. He was still having to rely on a wheelchair, but the day he began hormone therapy, I swear, he stood as tall as I. He has also commenced on a programme of surgery to complete the process. In comparison to the trauma faced by so many transpeople who present society with the truth it would rather not know, my brother's transition has run a relatively smooth path in recent years. His male identity is fully accepted, both by those who did not know his history and by those who do. In the latter group, those who knew him in his false, pre-transition disguise, the consensus has been that they "always knew" his androgyny would lead to the point he has reached now.

My brother does not deliberately choose to live "stealth" in every aspect of his life... for instance he made a point of "coming out" to his friends and colleagues at the university where he has worked for some of the time since transition. This revelation was greeted with surprise, but total support and admiration for his courage. In other situations, he lives his life as the man he is without explanations to anyone.

My brother lives with his female partner and other family, leading an ordered, normal existence, in stark contrast to the turmoil and disjointedness of his childhood and early youth. As far as I am concerned, gender identity is a fixed code, programmed before birth. The intense conditioning imposed by society may lead some into the confusion of denial, but most transpeople eventually have to respond in some way to the urgings of their true selves.

The reasons for my brother's androgyny lie in medical fact . (We suspect maternal medication for renal disease and the threat of miscarriage during pregnancy, but this is not certain.) The causative factors of gender dysphoria (although my brother always insists that he is quite happy with his gender ... it is society that seems to have the dysphoria) are multiple. There is a body of opinion that holds the theory that all transpeople are intersexed in some way.

Whatever the truth, it is the brain that makes the final decision and from this decision arises a no-choice scenario. Transpeople do not choose to be so, any more than others choose to have any other congenital condition. The only choice is to suffer or follow one's identity to its logical conclusion. The only group with free choice is the public at-large, who can choose to accept or deny the rights of this large minority group to a life worth living, free of bigotry and condemnation.

Friends ask me what my reaction was to finding out that my brother was "transsexual". I tell them that I always knew his identity, just as he did. The only transition in our lives has been the move away from pain and secrecy to the position of pride in how he has survived and thrived.

GLOSSARY OF TRANSGENDERED TERMS

Crossdresser: Someone who feels the need to express his or her other gender, at least part-time. Usually refers to heterosexual males, but there are females who crossdress as well. Former term: transvestite.

FTM or MTF: Transgendered persons may be female-to-male or male-to-female.

Gender: The traditional social concept that everyone is either male or female, usually based on the infant's genitalia, but also including many social and sexual role prescriptions.

Gender Dysphoria: Feelings of pain, anguish, and anxiety that arise from the mismatch between a trans person's physical sex and his or her internal gender identity.

Gender Identity: One's own personal sense of being a man or a woman, or a boy or a girl, or, occasionally, inbetween.

Gender Transition: The period when transsexual (and sometimes transgenderist) persons change their bodies in order to facilitate living their lives in the social role congruent with their bodies.

Hormonal Sex Reassignment: Administration of estrogens (for male to female transsexuals) or androgens (for female to male transsexuals) to promote the development of secondary sexual characteristics of the other sex.

Intersexed: The preferred term for persons born with ambiguous genitalia and/or chromosomal anomalies. Many intersexed infants and children have their ambiguous genitalia surgically "normalized" (altered), often resulting in the loss of sexual response and/or assignment to the wrong gender. Former term: Hermaphrodite.

Real Life Test (RLT): (also called the Real Life Experience) The one-year minimum period when transsexual persons must be able to demonstrate to their psychotherapist their ability to live successfully and work full-time in their congruent gender, a prerequisite for sex reassignment surgery (SRS), as mandated by the Standards of Care.

Sex: The state of biological maleness or femaleness identified at birth, as opposed to gender identity, which children seem to experience, or self-identify, at a very early age.

Sex Reassignment: Hormonal and surgical modification of the body to make it, as much as possible, like that of the other sex, in order to facilitate living in the social role matching one's gender identity.

Sex Reassignment Surgery (SRS): Permanent surgical refashioning of the genitalia to resemble the external genitalia of the other sex.

Sexual Orientation: Sexual attraction to persons of the same, opposite, or either sex. A person may be heterosexual, homosexual, bisexual, or asexual.

Si, Hir: New pronouns coined to avoid the male/female dichotomy, Si replaces she/he and hir replaces him/her.

SOFFA: A recently coined umbrella term referring to significant others, family members, friends and allies.

Standards of Care: A set of guidelines formulated by the Harry Benjamin International Gender Dysphoria Association intended to safeguard both transsexual persons and those who provide professional services.

140

Top surgery: Breast reduction for female-to-male transsexuals, as opposed to "bottom surgery," or genital reshaping.

Transgendered: Any person whose gender identity, expression, or behaviors are not traditionally associated with their birth sex. While not accepted by everyone, this term is widely used to designate the full spectrum of people with gender issues. (Other forms include transgenders or trans persons.)

Transgenderists: A term often used to refer to those transgendered persons, usually MTF, who choose to live full-time in the other gender without benefit of surgery or, sometimes, even hormones. Other terms: Non-op or non-operative transsexual.

Transsexuals: People who are profoundly unhappy in their birth sex and who seek to change, or have already changed, their bodies to match their gender identity. They may be FTM or MTF.

~~~~~~~~~~
Always be a first-rate version of yourself, instead of a second-rate version of somebody else.
— Judy Garland (from Raquel Rice)

REFERENCES AND PERMISSIONS

1. One exception may be Mariette Pathy Allen's beautiful book, *Transformations: Crossdressers and Those Who Love Them*, E. P. Dutton, Inc., 1989. Out of print; order from the author at: 100 Riverside Drive, #15A, New York, NY 10024, 212/496-0655.

2. Our Trans Children, published by PFLAG's Transgender Special Outreach Network (TSON), 1998. A 14 page introduction to transdender issues. Available from this author; see last page.

3. From Just Evelyn, *Mom, I Need To Be a Girl*, Walter Trook Publishing, 1998. Order from: Just Evelyn, 3707 Fifth Ave., #413, San Diego, CA 92103, 1-800-666-8158, www:justevelyn.com, $10, including postage and handling.

4. Some of the art work appeared in ARTherapy: Journal of the American Art Therapy Association. 1996 Vol. 13, No. 4, "A Mother's Journey of Healing: When a Child Changes Gender."

5. This article originally appeared in the author's email newsletter "Our Gender Family" edition #9 of January, 1998.

6. Abridged from article of same title, Chrysalis: The Journal of Transgressive Gender Identities, Fall 1997/Winter/1998, an issue devoted to intersexuality, American Educational Gender Information, merged but reachable at: P. O. Box 33724, Decatur, GA 30033-0724 or aegis@gender.org.

7. Just Evelyn, 1998.

NATIONAL TRANGENDER ORGANIZATIONS (12/98)

1. The American Boyz has local affiliates for female to male transgendered persons and their significant others, friends, family members and allies(SOFFAs). The American Boyz, P.O. Box 1118, Elkton, MD 21921. Website: www.netgsi.com/~listwrangler. Email: transman@netgsi.com.

2. FTM International provides support and information for female-to-male transsexuals. FTM International, 1360 Mission Street, Suite 200, San Francisco, CA 94103. Phone: (415) 553-5987. Website: www.ftm-intl.org. Email: TSTGMen@aol.com.

3. Gender Education and Advocacy (GEA) is a new national organization formed from the merger of AEGIS and It's Time, America! GEA, P.O. Box 65, Kensington, MD 20895. Phone: (301) 949-3822, voice mail box #8. Website: www.gender.org

4. The Gender Political Advocacy Coalition works for gender, affectional, and racial equality. GenderPAC, 733 15th Street NW, 7th Floor, Washington, DC 20005. Phone: (202) 347-3024. Website: www.gpac.org.

5. The Harry Benjamin International Gender Dysphoria Association, Inc. (HBIGDA), 1300 South 2nd Street, Suite 180, Minnesota, MN 55454, (612) 625-1500 provides the "Standards of Care", a guide for professionals treating transsexuals.

6. The International Conference on Transgender Law and Employment Policy (ICTLEP) provides legal referrals and information regarding redocumentation, family law and other legal issues of transgendered persons. Proceedings of their previous conferences are available. ICTLEP, P.O. Box 1010, Cooperstown, NY 13326. Phone (607) 547-4118. Email: ICTLEPHDQ@aol.com.

7. The International Foundation for Gender Education (IFGE) provides information, referrals and books. They also publish the quarterly magazine, Transgender. IFGE, PO Box 229, Waltham, MA 02454-0229.

Phone: (781) 899-2212. Website: www.transgender.org/tg/ifge. Email: IFGE@world.std.com

8. The Intersex Society of North America (ISNA) provides information and support, primarily for intersexed persons. ISNA, P.O. Box 31791, San Francisco, CA 94131. Email: info@isna.org

9. The National Youth Advocacy Coalition (NYAC) focuses on advocacy, education and information for gay, lesbian, bisexual, transgender and questioning youth. NYAC, 1711 Connecticut Avenue, NW, Suite 206, Washington, DC 20009-1139. Phone: (202) 319-7596. Email: NYouthAC@aol.com

10. PFLAG (Parents, Families, and Friends of Lesbians and Gays), provides support, education, and advocacy for GLBT persons and families in every state through its 410 affiliates and chapters. PFLAG, 1101 14th St., NW, Suite 1030, Washington DC 20005. Phone: (202) 638-4200. Website: http://www.pflag.org. Email: Info@pflag.org.

11. PFLAG's Transgender Special Outreach Network (TSON) focuses on information and support for both trans persons and their families. For personal questions or to join the list for parents of young gender variant children: (216) 691-4357 (HELP) or KittenGR@aol.com. For email information and support, send the message — subscribe TGS-PFLAG (and your email address)— to: listproc@Youth-Guard.org or contact the list owner at: raquel@yellowline.com.

12. The Renaissance Transgender Association, with chapters and affiliates throughout the US, provides support, education, and social outlet for crossdressers and others. Renaissance Transgender Association, 987 Old Eagle School Rd., Suite 719, Wayne, Pa USA 19087. Phone: (610) 975-9119. Email: bensalem@cpcn.com or rea@cdspub.com.

13. The Society for the Second Self (Tri-Ess) focuses on the needs of heterosexual crossdressers, and has about 30 chapters around the country. Tri-Ess, P.O. Box 194 Tulare, CA 93275.

N.B. Inquire at any of the above for other local and national groups.

BRIEF TRANSGENDER READING LIST

Bornstein, Kate, *Gender Outlaw: On Men, Women and the Rest of Us*. New York: Routledge, 1994.

Brown, Mildred and Rounsley, Chloe Ann, *True Selves: Understanding Transsexualism for Family, Friends, Coworkers and Helping Professionals*. San Francisco: Jossey-Bass, 1996.

Bullough, Vernon and Bullough, Bonnie, *Crossdressing, Sex and Gender*. Philadelphia: University of Pennsylvania Press, 1993.

Burke, Phyllis, Gender Shock: *Exploding the Myths of Male and Female*. New York: Doubleday, 1996.

Cameron, Loren, *Body Alchemy: Transsexual Portraits*. San Francisco: Cleis Press, 1996.

Ettner, Randi, *Confessions of a Gender Defender: A Psychologist's Reflections on Life Among the Transgendered*. Evanston, IL: Chicago Spectrum, 1996.

Feinberg, Leslie, *Transgendered Warriors: Making History from Joan of Arc to RuPaul*. Boston: Beacon Press, 1996.

Kirk, Sheila and Rothblatt, *Martine, Medical, Legal and Workplace Issues for the Transsexual*. Watertown, MA: Together Lifeworks, 1995.

Israel, Gianna and Tarver, D., *Transgender Care: Recommended Guidelines, Practical Information, and Personal Accounts*. Philadelphia: Temple University Press, 1997.

Rudd, Peggy, *Crossdressers and Those Who Share Their Lives.* Katy, TX: PM Publishers, 1995.

Stuart, Kim, *The Uninvited Dilemma: A Question of Gender.* Portland, OR: Metamorphous Press, 1983.

Sullivan, Lou, *Information for the Female-To-Male Cross-dresser and Transsexual.* Seattle: Ingersoll Gender Center, 1990.

See also References and Permissions.

HOW TO ORDER THIS BOOK

You may order copies of this book from the editor, Mary Boenke. Make checks payable to her and send to her at: 180 Bailey Blvd., Hardy, VA 24101. For further information: 540/890-3957, maryboenke@aol.com, or www.aiyiyi.com/transbook.

The cost is $13.95, including shipping and mailing, for one through three books. Inquire about cost for quantity orders.

P.S.

I would be glad to hear from readers who have found this book helpful, who have corrections and suggestions, or who have stories of their own to tell. I will forward letters to any of this volume's contributors. MMB